HEINEMANN HISTORY

THE ERA OF THE SECOND WORLD WAR

STUDY UNITS

Nigel Kelly
Martyn Whittock

Heinemann

Heinemann Library,
an imprint of Heinemann Educational,
a division of Heinemann Publishers (Oxford) Ltd,
Halley Court, Jordan Hill, Oxford OX2 8EJ

OXFORD   LONDON   EDINBURGH   MADRID
ATHENS   BOLOGNA   PARIS   MELBOURNE
SYDNEY   AUCKLAND   SINGAPORE   TOKYO
IBADAN   NAIROBI   HARARE   GABORONE
PORTSMOUTH NH (USA)

First published 1993

97 96 95 94 93

10 9 8 7 6 5 4 3 2 1

**British Library Cataloguing in Publication Data is available from
the British Library on request.**

ISBN 0–431–07356–2

Designed by Ron Kamen, Green Door Design Ltd, Basingstoke

Illustrated by Phill Burrows and Jeff Edwards

Printed in Spain by Mateu Cromo

The cover shows children sheltering during a bombing raid.

Acknowledgements

The authors and publisher would like to thank the following
for permission to reproduce photographs:
Bilderdienst Suddeutscher Verlag: 4.3D; Bridgeman Art
Library/Imperial War Museum: 1.1A; British Library: 1.2A;
Centre for the Study of Cartoons and Caricature: 3.2C; Centre
for the Study of Cartoons and Caricature/David Low/Solo
Syndication: 4.8D; Collection of Gunn Brinson: 1.4A; E. T.
Archive: 1.1C, 4.3A, 4.7F; Mary Evans Picture Library: 1.4F,
4.7A; Hulton-Deutsch Collection: 1.4G, 2.5E, 4.4D, 4.6C;
L'Illustration/Sygma: 2.2A; Imperial War Museum: 2.7A,
3.1A, 3.3A, 4.1B, 4.3H, 4.4C, 4.5B; Library of Congress,
Washington: 4.8C; National Air and Space Museum,
Smithsonian Institution: 3.5D; Netherlands Photo
Archive/Charles Breijer: 4.2C; Popperfoto: 1.4D, 2.2C, 2.3A,
2.5A, 4.5E, 5.1D; The Prado, Madrid © DACS 1993/Arxiu
Mas: 2.4B; Sygma: p.56, p.57; Topham Picture Source: Cover,
3.2A; Weimar Archive: 1.4C, 3.4B.
We are also grateful to the following for permission to repro-
duce copyright material:
Collins Educational for Source 5.2A, taken from P. Moss,
History Alive, 1977.

Every effort has been made to contact copyright holders of
material reproduced in this book. Any omissions will be recti-
fied in subsequent printings if notice is given to the publisher.

Thanks to Dr Steven Constantine for his comments on the
manuscript.

To Tutor Group 987, the dedication I promised you. MW

Details of written sources

In some sources the wording or sentence structure has been
simplified to ensure that the source is accessible.

S. L. Case, *The Second World War*, Evans Brothers, 1981: 3.4A
B. Catchpole, *A Map History of the Modern World*, Heinemann
Educational, 1982: 1.3A, 2.1A, 4.8A, 5.3F
A. Cobban, *A History of Modern France*, Pelican, 1961: 1.4E
Margaret Costa, 'Reliving 1946: The Food Front', *Sunday
Times*, 2 May 1965: 4.4A
Chris Culpin, *Making History*, Collins, 1984: 4.7C, 4.8F
B. Elliot, *Hitler and Germany*, Longman, 1966: 1.3B, 2.2D,
2.5D
P. Fisher and N. Williams, *Past into Present, Book 3*, Collins,
1989: 2.2B
History of the Second World War, Purnell, 1968: 3.5B, 4.2B
T. Howarth, *The World Since 1900*, Longman, 1979: 4.3E
T. Howarth, *Twentieth Century History*, Longman, 1979: 2.7C
Illustrated London News, April 1936: 2.3D, 2.3E
Illustrated London News, March 1939: 2.4C
Nigel Kelly, *The Second World War*, Heinemann Educational,
1989: 3.3B, 3.5C, 4.3B, 4.3C, 4.3G, 4.6B, 4.6D, 4.8G, 5.3E
Stephen Lee, *Nazi Germany*, Heinemann Educational, 1989:
2.6E, 4.7E
Peter Mantin, *The Twentieth Century World*, Hutchinson,
1987: 4.3F
Karl Marx, *The Communist Manifesto*, Penguin Edition, 1967:
1.4B
C. K. McDonald, *The Second World War*, Blackwell, 1984:
3.5A, 4.4B
Peter Moss, *Modern World History*, Hart-Davis Educational,
1978: 2.3B, 5.2C
Novosti Press Agency, *Recalling the Past*, Moscow, 1985: 2.6G
Alastair and Anne Pike, *The Home Front: Oral and
Contemporary Accounts*, Tressol, 1985: 4.5A, 4.5C
J. Roberts, *History of the World*, Pelican, 1980: 1.3C
Joe Scott, *The World Since 1914*, Heinemann Educational,
1989: 2.4A, 4.1A, 5.1B, 5.2D
R. Seth, *Operation Barbarossa*, Blond, 1964: 3.2B
K. Shephard, *International Relations, 1919–39*, Blackwell, 1987:
1.1B, 1.1D, 1.4H, 2.1C, 2.1D, 2.4D, 2.7D, 2.7E, 2.7F
Paul Shuter and Terry Lewis, *Skills in History, Book 3*,
Heinemann Educational, 1988: 2.1E, 4.8B
John Simkin, *Contemporary Account of the Second World War*,
Tressel Publications, 1984: 3.1B, 4.2A, 4.2B, 4.3I
L. Snellgrove, *The Modern World Since 1870*, Longman, 1981:
2.5B, 2.5C, 2.6F, 5.1A, 5.1C
A. J. P. Taylor, *The Origins of World War Two*, Hamish
Hamilton, 1963: 2.3C
Ben Wicks, *No Time to Wave Goodbye*, Bloomsbury, 1988:
4.5D, 4.5F

CONTENTS

1.1 The War to End All Wars

The First World War ended in 1918. It was the most costly war that had ever been fought, in terms of both casualties and money. Between 1914 and 1918, **20 million people** had died as a result of the war, nine million in combat, and the countries involved had spent a total of £35,448 million. At the time people called it the 'Great War' and even 'the war to end all wars'.

The incredible cost in lives and resources exhausted many of the countries involved. The First World War was a **total war**. This means that it affected the lives of civilians as well as soldiers. The entire **economies** of many of the countries involved had to be centred on fighting the war. The British used the resources of their Empire. Over 200,000 Empire soldiers died; one-third of these were from India. Some countries also faced unrest during the war. Parts of the French army mutinied in 1917. The same year, Britain had to deal with a rising in Ireland and there was a revolution in Russia. German soldiers and sailors mutinied in 1918.

'Hell', a contemporary painting by the French artist Georges Leroux. It shows a First World War battlefield.

B SOURCE

Last night for the first time since August in the first year of the war there was no light of gunfire in the sky, no stabs of flame through darkness, where for four years human beings were smashed to death. The fires of hell had been put out.

The US journalist Philip Gibbs, writing in 'The New York Times', November 1918.

C

LES ASSASSINS REVIENNENT TOUJOURS...

...SUR LES LIEUX DE LEUR CRIME

French poster of 1919 showing the horrors of the war and the destruction that it caused to France.

D

Millions of people were unemployed; returning soldiers could not find work, and others lost their jobs when factories stopped making weapons. In some countries, money lost its value. Much of the European railway system was in ruins. Production of grain and coal was low and people were starving in Germany and Austria.

K. Shephard, 'International Relations 1919–39', 1987.

Haig

Douglas Haig (1851–1928) was born in Edinburgh. He served in the Sudan and South Africa, before becoming Commander-in-Chief of the British Forces on the Western Front in 1915. He masterminded the First World War strategy of trench warfare which resulted in appalling casualties at the Somme (1916) and Passchendaele (1917). His apparent disregard for human life earned him the nickname 'the Butcher' among his troops.

After the war, in 1919, Haig was made an Earl and set up the 'Poppy Day' appeal to help wounded soldiers. He died in 1928.

Many areas were wrecked by the fighting. These included north-east France, much of Belgium, north-east Italy and western Russia. It was tremendously expensive to rebuild these areas.

The terrible casualties of the war were caused by new weapons of warfare. Machine guns, aeroplanes, long-range artillery, tanks and poison gas were weapons used in the fighting. Human lives were destroyed by new technology.

In many countries people felt that such an event should never happen again. Some of these people were known as **pacifists**. They believed that violence was always wrong.

1.2 The Price of Peace

Europe after the Peace Treaties of 1919–20.

- Territory lost by Germany to other countries
- Territory lost by Germany to the League of Nations
- Area formerly Austria–Hungary
- Territory lost by Russia
- Demilitarized zone

N

NORWAY

SWEDEN

FINLAND

RUSSIA

ESTONIA

LATVIA

LITHUANIA

Northern Schleswig lost to Denmark

DENMARK

Danzig (free city run by the League)

MEMEL

EAST PRUSSIA

WEST PRUSSIA

Small, weak states helpless against Russian power

3,000,000 Germans lived in the Sudetenland, now part of Czechoslovakia

GREAT BRITAIN

NETHERLANDS

Elbe

BELGIUM

Berlin

POSEN

G E R M A N Y

P O L A N D

East Prussia separated from Germany by the 'Polish corridor'

Germany lost Eupen and Malmedy to Belgium

Weimar

Rhine

Oder

Germany lost this to Poland

Germany lost all its colonies. Many Germans returned from colonies to Germany

RUSSIA

Versailles • Paris

C Z E C H O S L O V A K I A

SILESIA

Saar coalfields were placed under French rule for five years

ALSACE AND LORRAINE

Danube

Germany was forbidden to unite with Austria

AUSTRIA

HUNGARY

ROMANIA

F R A N C E

Germany lost Alsace and Lorraine to France (which had lost them to Germany in 1871)

Austria and Hungary now two separate, land-locked countries

YUGOSLAVIA

BULGARIA

SPAIN

I T A L Y

ALBANIA

GREECE

TURKEY

0   300 miles

0   400 km

The countries which had won the First World War (the **Allies**) were determined to make sure that nothing like it would ever happen again. They tried to deal with the problems that might threaten peace in the future. Before the war Germany, Austria-Hungary, Turkey and Russia had ruled empires. These empires had fallen apart by 1918. The victorious Allies wanted to make sure that these countries could never become so powerful again. The map of Europe was re-drawn. Smaller nations were given the right to govern themselves. Austria and Hungary became two different countries. New countries like **Yugoslavia** and **Czechoslovakia** were set up in areas once part of the great empires. **Poland** was re-formed from areas ruled by Russia, Austria-Hungary and Germany.

In 1919 the victorious Allies signed the **Treaty of Versailles** with Germany. Many Germans were angered by the Treaty and called it a **diktat** – a decision forced upon them against their wishes. The Germans were forced to admit blame for the war (the **war guilt** clause). They would have to pay for the damage caused during the war (**reparations**). Their once mighty army was limited to 100,000 men. They could have no tanks, submarines or warplanes. All the German colonies were taken away from them. They lost land that they had controlled in Europe in 1914. They were forbidden to ever unite with Austria as one country (known as **Anschluss**). In the end the Germans had lost 13% of their land in Europe, 12% of their population, 16% of their coal mines and 48% of their iron works.

The Peace Treaties and defeated countries		
1919	Treaty of Versailles	Germany
1919	Treaty of St Germain	Austria
1919	Treaty of Neuilly	Bulgaria
1920	Treaty of Trianon	Hungary
1920	Treaty of Sèvres	Turkey
This treaty was not signed.		
1923	Treaty of Lausanne	Turkey

PEACE AND FUTURE CANNON FODDER

The Tiger: "Curious! I seem to hear a child weeping!"

Cartoon drawn by Will Dyson in 1919. The four leaders are, from left to right, Lloyd George (Britain), Orlando (Italy), 'Tiger' Clemenceau (France) and Wilson (USA). Children who were babies in 1919 would be the soldiers of 1940.

Lloyd-George

David Lloyd-George (1863–1945) first entered politics as Liberal MP for Caernarvon in 1890, a seat he held for 55 years. During the Liberal Government of 1908–16 he was Chancellor of the Exchequer. He helped introduce a series of social reforms such as the Old Age Pensions Act (1908). In 1916 he became Prime Minister of a coalition government. After the war he represented Britain at the Versailles peace conference. In 1922 he resigned as Prime Minister though he remained in Parliament until 1945.

1.3 The League of Nations

The League of Nations was the idea of the President of the USA, **Woodrow Wilson**. The aim of this organization was to encourage the countries of the world to work together. He hoped that they might sort out their problems by discussion (**negotiation**) instead of by fighting. He also hoped that the League could help reduce the numbers of weapons made by the countries of the world.

Wilson hoped that the League would give **collective security** to its members – that is, countries would stand together and protect each other. If a country attacked a member of the League, the other members could stop trading with the attacker. This is known as **applying sanctions**. If this did not work then the League countries could send soldiers to help beat off the attack. The League would also do things such as help **refugees**, and help stop **slavery** and **drug addiction**. After the First World War, the defeated countries lost their empires. Some of these areas were governed by the victorious Allies on behalf of the League. They were called **mandates**.

A **SOURCE**

The League never truly had world support and quickly turned into a talking shop, dominated by countries which won World War I. At times they were able to bully small countries into submission; but they were powerless to influence the other great nations.

B. Catchpole, 'A Map History of the Modern World', 1982.

The structure of the League of Nations.

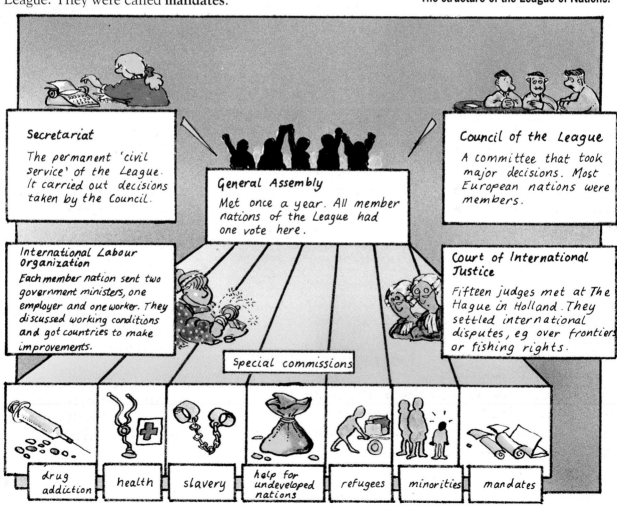

Secretariat
The permanent 'civil service' of the League. It carried out decisions taken by the Council.

General Assembly
Met once a year. All member nations of the League had one vote here.

Council of the League
A committee that took major decisions. Most European nations were members.

International Labour Organization
Each member nation sent two government ministers, one employer and one worker. They discussed working conditions and got countries to make improvements.

Court of International Justice
Fifteen judges met at The Hague in Holland. They settled international disputes, eg over frontiers or fishing rights.

Special commissions

drug addiction | health | slavery | help for undeveloped nations | refugees | minorities | mandates

The League was set up in 1920. Between 50 and 60 countries were eventually members.

In 1921 the **Court of International Justice** was set up by the League in the city of **The Hague**, in the Netherlands. It had fifteen judges from different countries. Governments could bring their disputes to Court and the judges would decide who was right or wrong, and how the dispute could be settled.

The League paid for the **International Labour Organization**. This encouraged governments to provide better wages and working conditions for workers in their country. This did lead to some improvements.

The League had some successes. In 1920 it helped settle a dispute between Sweden and Finland about who should govern the **Aaland Islands** in the Baltic. In the same year the League settled a dispute between Yugoslavia and Albania and divided an area called Upper Silesia which both Germany and Poland thought they should have. In 1925 it helped sort out a disagreement between Bulgaria and Greece over their frontier. It raised money to help Austria which was facing great financial problems after losing the war. In 1932 the League settled a border dispute between Peru and Colombia.

However, the League had many problems. Although President Wilson was in favour of it, he lost power and the USA did not join. This greatly weakened the League. The USSR was not allowed to join until 1934. Germany was finally allowed to join in 1926 but in 1933 Hitler took Germany out of the League. In over 22 years only 32 disputes came before the Court of International Justice. Most governments wanted to settle their disagreements themselves. This meant that the meetings of different ambassadors (the **Conference of Ambassadors**) came to be more important.

In 1919 Poland used force to take the city of **Vilna** from Lithuania. The League protested but the Conference of Ambassadors let the Poles get away with it. In 1923 the Lithuanians used force to seize the German port of **Memel**. The League protested but did not stop them. In 1923 Italy attacked and seized the Greek island of **Corfu**. The Conference of Ambassadors ordered the Greeks to give in to the more powerful Italians. Many countries were not prepared to use force against those who threatened the peace.

SOURCE B

Lacking the support of the USA, the USSR until 1934 and Germany after 1933 the League was unable to prevent fighting and squabbling in many parts of the world.

B. Elliott, 'Hitler and Germany', 1966.

SOURCE C

The League was to have its successes in usefully handling matters which might without its intervention have proved dangerous.

J. Roberts, 'History of the World', 1980.

Wilson

Woodrow Wilson (1856–1924) was elected President of the USA in 1912. He kept his country out of the First World War until 1917. Towards the end of the war he issued his '14 Points' as a basis for peace talks, and represented the USA at Versailles, where he proposed a 'League of Nations' should be set up. However, he could not persuade the Americans to join. In 1919 he had a stroke while campaigning for support for the League in the USA. He was an invalid until his death in 1924.

1.4 Power and Politics

A German Communist poster from 1920. Its message is 'Vote Spartacist' and overthrow the government.

During the 1920s and '30s different groups of people had competing ideas about how countries should be governed. There was often violence between people who disagreed about these **political ideas**. Many of the problems of the time were caused by such rivalries.

One of the main political beliefs is **democracy**. In a democracy people choose their own government by voting for representatives. In these countries, different **political parties** compete for people's votes. People are allowed to express their opinion about how the country should be run. Newspapers can print stories in favour of or against the government. Countries such as **Britain**, **France** and the **USA** were democracies throughout the 1920s and '30s, and continue to have a democratic style of government.

Some people disagreed with the ideas of democracy. They believed that power should be held by only some of the people; that a country should be controlled by one leader or a small group of people. The person who holds this kind of power is often called a **dictator**.

Let the ruling classes tremble at a Communist revolution. The working class have nothing to lose but their chains. They have a world to win. Working men of all countries unite!

K. Marx, 'The Communist Manifesto', 1848.

A German anti-Communist poster from the 1920s. It shows Communism as bringing death and disaster.

Marx

Karl Marx was born in Trier in Germany in 1818. He attended universities in Berlin and Bonn where he studied philosophy and history. From 1843 he became involved with groups opposed to the government. As a result he was forced to move from Germany, first to Paris and then to Brussels. With another famous philosopher, Friedrich Engels, he wrote the *Communist Manifesto* which encouraged workers to overthrow their rulers.

In order to avoid imprisonment as a revolutionary Marx was forced to flee to London. There he lived in poverty, while carrying out research for his book *Das Kapital*. In this book he wrote that there should be no social classes, but that everyone should have an equal share of wealth and power. These views are the basis of modern Communism, which established itself in Russia in 1917. Marx died in England in 1883 and is buried in Highgate cemetery, London.

In the 1920s and '30s many people supported **Marxism**, or **Communism**. The ideas of **Karl Marx** had been adopted by **Vladimir Lenin** in Russia. They believed that the people who worked in the mines and factories (the **proletariat** or **working class**) should destroy the power of the rich people who owned land and factories (the **capitalists** or **ruling class**). Communists believed that everyone should have an equal share of power and wealth.

In 1917 **Bolsheviks** (as the Russian Communists called themselves) had seized power in Russia in the **Russian Revolution** and created the USSR. There were strong Communist parties in France and Germany. For a short while in 1919 German Communists managed to seize power in a part of Germany called Bavaria. Other German Communists (called **Spartacists**) tried to lead a revolution in Berlin. In 1919 an organization was set up to try to encourage Communist revolutions across the world. It was named the **Comintern**.

Short-lived Communist revolts, 1918–19.

SOURCE D

Dr Dollfuss, the leader of the Austrian Fascist party (the Heimwehr) at a rally in Vienna in 1934.

Fascists believed in **totalitarianism** like many Communists. In a totalitarian system, a single person or a political party controls all activities, either political or otherwise, and does not allow any opposition parties to exist. However there were serious differences between the two groups. Communists believed that working people should not care about what country they belonged to. All they should care about was what **class** they belonged to. They should unite with workers from other countries to get rid of the capitalists. This is called **internationalism**. The Fascists thought that it was very important which country a person belonged to. They believed in **nationalism**.

The front cover of 'La Tribuna Illustrata', showing Hitler and Mussolini at a parade in Berlin, 1937.

Fascists thought that people should be very proud of their country. They were **racist**: they believed in the superiority of their own race and were **prejudiced** against people from different ethnic groups.

SOURCE E

On 6 February 1934 the right wing groups [Fascists] called out their forces. They attacked the Chamber of Deputies [the French parliament]. Armed police held them off and killed fourteen of the demonstrators.

A. Cobban, 'A History of Modern France', 1961.

SOURCE F

LA TRIBUNA ILLUSTRATA

LA STORICA VISITA DEL DUCE AL FÜHRER
I due Condottieri acclamati dal grande popolo tedesco

Mosley, the leader of the British Fascists, in Liverpool, 1937.

H

SOURCE

Your rights? What rubbish! Here I can arrest anyone that I want to and I can keep them in prison for as long as I want to.

The Head of the Portugese Secret Police – the PVDE – speaking to an opponent of the Portugese Fascist government.

The first Fascists came from Italy. Their leader was **Benito Mussolini**. He governed Italy from 1922 until 1943. Other Fascists – called the **Nazis** – took power in Germany in 1933.

Fascists from different countries had many things in common. They all believed in being ruled by a strong leader or dictator. In Italy Mussolini was called **Il Duce**. In Germany **Hitler** was called **Der Führer**. Both these titles mean 'The Leader'. Both dictators banned other political parties and used violence to get rid of opposition. All Fascists were in favour of having a strong army and they all hated Communists.

Other dictators took power in other European countries. These included **Admiral Horthy** in Hungary (1920), **Marshal Pilsudski** in Poland (1926), **Dr Dollfuss** and later **Dr Schuschnigg** in Austria (1932 and 1934), and **General Metaxas** in Greece (1936). Fascists took power in Portugal in 1932 and in Spain in 1939. Other rulers who restricted freedom were **King Alexander** of Yugoslavia (1929), **King Boris** of Bulgaria (1934), and **King Carol** of Romania (1937).

Not all Fascists succeeded in taking power in the countries where they were active. There were Fascist organizations in France such as *Solidarité Française* and *Action Française*. In Belgium the Fascists were called **Rexists**. In Britain the **British Union of Fascists** was led by **Oswald Mosley**. In these countries not enough people supported the Fascists for them to gain power; the countries stayed as democracies.

Mussolini

Benito Mussolini (1883–1940) was the son of a blacksmith. In 1902 he left Italy to avoid army service. When he returned in 1904 he became an active socialist. In 1914 he was expelled from the Socialist Party because he wanted Italy to take part in the First World War. In 1919 he set up the Fascist Party and in 1922 became Prime Minister. By 1925 'Il Duce' (the Leader) had established himself as dictator in Italy.

In 1940 he took Italy into the war to support his ally, Adolf Hitler. In 1943 he was overthrown, but rescued by the Germans. But in April 1945 he was captured by Italian partisans and shot. His body was hanged upside down in a square in Milan.

2.1 The Japanese Attack on Manchuria

During the 1930s there were a number of threats to world peace. Looking back, many modern historians describe these as being steps which led to the Second World War. At the time, of course, people were not aware of where these events were leading.

Japan was keen to become more powerful in Asia. The Japanese had defeated the Russians in a war fought in 1904–5 and had taken control of **Korea** in 1910. They also had an army in **Manchuria** (part of China) to protect the railway line there. During the 1920s there was **civil war** in **China**. This weakened China and encouraged some Japanese leaders to try to seize more land there.

Japan wanted more land for a number of reasons. The Japanese population had risen to 97 million; there were not enough jobs for all these people in Japan. Japanese industries needed more **raw materials** like iron ore, wool, aluminium and rubber. The Japanese could use these to make goods and sell them abroad. After 1929 the economies of most of the countries of the world were in serious trouble. Many leaders of the Japanese army were keen to solve their economic problems by capturing land in Asia. The government found it difficult to control the army.

A **SOURCE**

The Manchurian affair had three very important results. First, it showed that the League of Nations was not capable of keeping world peace. Second, it encouraged the European dictators to try the same tactics in Africa and Europe. Third, the Japanese had no more hesitation about extending their empire by armed force.

B. Catchpole, 'A Map History of the Modern World', 1982.

In 1931 the Japanese army invaded Manchuria. It claimed that the Chinese had tried to destroy the railway line at **Mukden**. By the end of 1932 the Japanese had seized control of the area. They changed its name to **Manchukuo**. They set up a Chinese ruler to run it but kept real control themselves. Manchukuo was a **puppet state**.

China appealed to the League of Nations for help. The League sent a team to Manchuria to discover who was really to blame. This was called the **Lytton Enquiry**.

B **SOURCE**

Chinese casualties after a Japanese bombing raid during the Sino-Japanese war, 1931–36.

Japanese expansion in Asia in the 1930s.

Manchuria had raw materials: coal, oil, bauxite, iron ore. It offered new markets. It was also a good base for attacking China

Japan had a growing population (over 97 million). It needed raw materials for industry: iron, coal, aluminium and oil. It also needed new markets where it could sell what was made in Japan

Extent of Japanese occupation
- By 1920s
- 1931–2
- 1933
- 1935–6
- After 1937

In the end the Enquiry accused the Japanese. In 1933 Japan left the League because of this, but kept the land that it had captured from the Chinese.

In 1937 Japan launched a full invasion of China. The Japanese treated the Chinese civilians with tremendous violence and cruelty. Once more the Chinese appealed to the League of Nations for help. The League failed to take action. No other country was willing to stop trading with the Japanese or selling them weapons. By 1938 Japan controlled most of eastern China.

C Chinese troops damaged the tracks of the South Manchurian railway near Mukden and attacked our guards at midnight.

Official Japanese army report, 24 September 1931.

D At 10 o'clock last night Japanese railway guards picked a quarrel by blowing up a section of the railway line near Mukden and then accusing the Chinese of having done this.

Official Chinese report, 19 September 1931.

E The Japanese claimed that Chinese troops had provoked the attack by sabotaging a Japanese railway line. The Chinese denied this. The League of Nations Commission said it could find no evidence to support the Japanese story.

P. Shuter and T. Lewis, 'Skills in History', 1988.

Chiang Kai-shek

Chiang Kai-shek (1887–1975) was a Chinese political leader who came to power as head of the Kuomintang in the 1920s. After the overthrow of the Manchu Dynasty in 1911, Chiang helped defeat the warlords of northern China. He was fiercely anti-Communist and forced them to undertake the famous 'Long March' of 1934–35 to avoid extermination. Chiang fought against the Japanese in the Second World War and from 1945 was President of China. He was overthrown by the Communist leader Mao Tse-tung in 1949 and forced to flee from mainland China to the island of Taiwan. Here he set up a nationalist government but was unable to restore himself to power on the mainland.

2.2 Adolf Hitler – the Growing Threat

A SOURCE

Hitler in Saarbrucken, March 1935. Germans in the Saar voted to be returned to Germany.

In January 1933 Hitler became ruler of Germany. He was the leader of a political party called the **National Socialist** or **Nazi Party**. He was determined to get revenge for all of the losses that Germany had suffered as a result of the **Treaty of Versailles**. The Nazis wanted to make Germany a powerful military country once more. They also wanted to unite all Germans in Europe under their leadership. They believed that Germany needed *Lebensraum* ('living space') in order to expand and grow. To gain this, Germany must conquer more land in Europe.

Soon after Hitler came to power he began to increase secretly the size of the German army and navy. This was forbidden by the Treaty of Versailles. From 1933 the German *Luftwaffe* (airforce) began to build secretly the Dornier twin-engined bomber.

Later in 1933 Hitler left the League of Nations because it would not agree with his plans for rearming Germany. After this he openly increased German military strength. He introduced **conscription** (compulsory military service) aimed at increasing the size of the army to 500,000 men. New tanks, submarines and planes were built. In 1936 a new German battleship, named the **Admiral Graf Spee**, was launched.

B SOURCE

Serious economic problems between 1928 and 1933 made possible the rise of the Nazi Party led by Adolf Hitler. After gaining power Hitler dominated Germany and promised that his new prosperous and powerful German Reich [Empire] would last for 1000 years.

P. Fisher and N. Williams, 'Past into Present', 1989.

In 1934 Nazis in Austria tried to seize power. They killed Dr Dollfuss, the ruler of Austria. The Italian dictator Mussolini did not want to see Austria controlled by Germany. He moved troops to the border between Austria and Italy and warned Germany to keep out of Austria.

In March 1935 an area called the **Saar** voted to be returned to Germany. It had been separated from Germany since the end of the First World War. Now 90% of its population voted to go back to German control. This boosted Hitler's popularity; it also gave him more resources such as coal, iron and steel.

Later in March 1935 France, Britain and Italy agreed to stand together to control the growth of Hitler's Germany. This alliance was called the **Stresa Front**. The agreement was broken almost immediately by Britain. The British signed the **Anglo–German Naval Treaty** which agreed to a limited increase in the size of the German navy. In 1936 the Italians fell out with Britain and France over the Italian invasion of Abyssinia. The Stresa Front was in ruins.

Comments about Hitler from different British experts in the mid-1930s.

C

SOURCE

Hitler shortly after leaving the Disarmament Conference of the League of Nations, October 1933.

Stresemann

Gustav Stresemann (1878–1929) achieved fame in Germany in the 1920s for rescuing the country from its economic problems. He first entered the Reichstag in 1906 and from August–November 1923 he was Chancellor of Germany. He is best remembered for his work as Foreign Minister. He brought Germany into the League of Nations and signed the Locarno Pact with the other European powers. In 1926 he was awarded the Nobel Peace Prize. He also persuaded the Allies to agree to a reduction in the amount of reparation payments that Germany was making.

2.3 The Italian Invasion of Abyssinia, 1935

A SOURCE

An Italian photograph from 1935. It shows Abyssinians in the province of Tigre saluting their new ruler, Benito Mussolini.

B SOURCE

It is a question of the very existence of the League; of the value of the promise made to small states that their independence shall be respected. God and history will remember your judgement.

The Abyssinian Emperor Haile Selassie in a speech to the League of Nations, 1935.

C SOURCE

The real death of the League was in December 1935. One day it was a powerful body imposing sanctions; the next day it was an empty sham, everyone scuttling from it as quickly as possible.

A. J. P. Taylor, 'The Origins of the Second World War', 1961.

The Italian dictator Mussolini dreamed of building an empire in Africa. Other countries such as Britain and France already owned a lot of land in Africa. Mussolini hoped to do the same and build a new Roman Empire. He called the Mediterranean **'Mare Nostrum'** (**our sea**) and hoped to dominate the lands around it.

The Italians already ruled areas of north and east Africa. They controlled **Libya** in the north and **Eritrea** and **Italian Somaliland** in the east. The Italians wanted more land. They planned to invade **Abyssinia** (now known as **Ethiopia**). This country was not ruled by Europeans. It was ruled by a black African Emperor, **Haile Selassie**.

The Italians had attacked Abyssinia before, in 1896. Then they had been defeated by the Abyssinians at the **Battle of Adowa**.

D SOURCE

All our aeroplanes are being used to bomb and machine gun this disorderly mob.

The Italian commander Marshal Badoglio describing the Battle of Lake Ashangi, April 1936, where the Italians won.

In October 1935 the Italians attacked Abyssinia once more. This time they used the most up-to-date weapons such as poison gas and aircraft. Although the Abyssinians had few modern weapons they put up fierce resistance and suffered terrible casualties.

Abyssinia appealed to the League of Nations for help. On 7 October the League decided to impose **sanctions** on Italy. This meant stopping the sale of goods to them. However, the League did not include the sale of steel, copper or oil in these sanctions. These were just the kind of things the Italians needed to fight a war. The League's decision not to include them meant that Mussolini could carry on with his attack on Abyssinia.

The League did decide not to sell weapons to either side. But this also helped the Italians. They had lots of weapons already, whereas the Abyssinians were desperate to get hold of modern weapons. The League's decision meant that they could not buy any.

The British finally suggested that no more oil should be sold to Italy after December 1935. But soon, reports leaked out about a deal that the British and French governments were discussing. This promised Mussolini that if he stopped fighting he could keep what he had seized. The deal was called the **Hoare–Laval Pact**. This was so unpopular with people in France and Britain that it was never actually carried out. However it had showed that Britain and France would not stand up to Italy. They were afraid of opposing Mussolini in case Italy formed an alliance with Germany. In 1936 the Italians completed their conquest of Abyssinia.

Italy's invasion of Abyssinia, 1935–6.

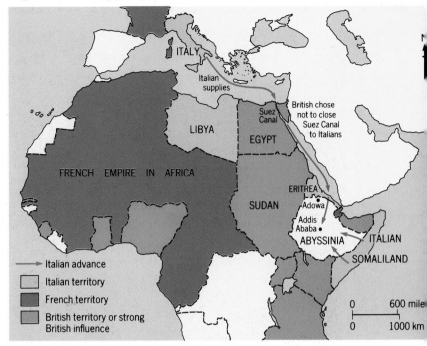

E

SOURCE

The Abyssinian losses were described as heavy and Italian casualties were about 40 dead and wounded. For five days there had been desperate attacks on the Italian positions against superior numbers, equipment and organization.

From the 'Illustrated London News', April 1936.

Haile Selassie

Haile Selassie (1892–1975) was born in Ethiopia as Ras (Prince) Tafari. In 1916 he led a successful revolution against the Ethiopian leader, Lij Yasu, and spent the next fourteen years as Regent for Princess Zauditu. When she died in 1930, he became Emperor. In 1935 he was driven from Ethiopia by an Italian invasion and made a passionate speech in the League of Nations asking for help. Restored to his throne in 1941, he was overthrown by a military coup in 1974 after years of poverty and starvation in Ethiopia. Yet to some Africans he is considered a religious figure. To Rastafarians, he is seen as a god.

2.4 The Spanish Civil War, 1936–39

In the early 1930s there was a lot of unrest in Spain. In the great industrial cities of **Barcelona** and **Bilbao** there were many unemployed workers. In the countryside there were over two million peasants who did not own their own land. These peasants, called **braceros**, were very poor. The unemployed and the poor resented the great wealth held by a minority of the people of Spain. This included the Roman Catholic Church which owned a lot of land and was very rich.

Many of the poorer people supported **left wing** political parties. These included **Communists** who wanted Spain to be ruled in the same way as the USSR, **Socialists** who wanted the government to share some of the wealth of the country among more people and **Anarchists** who wanted to get rid of all government.

King Alfonso XIII **abdicated** (resigned as king) in 1931. After this, Spain was a **Republic**. In 1936 elections led to the setting up of a **Popular Front** government. This was made up of a number of left wing parties. These people aimed to change Spain. They wanted to take land away from the Church, stop Church control of education, give land to poor peasants, give different areas of Spain their own governments and limit the

A

SOURCE

The Spanish government consisted of Socialists and Communists. General Franco, who led an army rebellion against them, held many of the same ideas as Hitler. Above all he was against Communism. Germany and Italy sent troops and supplies to Franco and this was probably the main reason for his success in 1939. The USSR sent some help to the Spanish government. The British and French decided to keep out.

J. Scott, 'The World Since 1914', 1989.

B

SOURCE

'Guernica', painted by Picasso in 1937. German planes bombed Guernica, a Republican town, in 1937 – this was the first major air raid against civilians in Europe. Picasso, a Spaniard who supported the Republic, used the painting to show the strength of feeling about the attack. Picasso was not actually present at Guernica during the bombing.

power of the army. Wealthy Spaniards feared the changes.

On 17 July 1936 leading Spanish army generals rebelled against the Republican Government. They took control of Spanish land in North Africa and also attempted to seize power in Spain itself. They were led by **General Franco**.

The revolt led to a bloody **civil war** which lasted until 1939. Although the main countries of Europe agreed not to get involved, the USSR sent help to the Republicans, and Germany and Italy sent help to Franco. German planes were used to bomb Spanish cities. Britain and France kept out as they were afraid that the war might spread to other parts of Europe if they took sides.

In 1939 the last Republican attempt to defeat Franco was beaten. In March 1939 Madrid surrendered to Franco.

C SOURCE

General Franco entered Madrid without a shot being fired. The city was occupied by troops led by the Italian General Gambara, who was welcomed by cheering crowds. Perhaps the most welcome sight to the inhabitants were the lorries from which food was given to the hungry crowds.

From the 'Illustrated London News', March 1939.

D SOURCE

Mussolini hoped Franco would be a useful ally. Hitler hoped a war in Spain would distract Mussolini from a German takeover in Austria and he saw Franco as an ally against France. He also used the Spanish war to test out German weapons.

K. Shephard, 'International Relations 1919–39', 1987.

Areas captured by General Franco and the Nationalists by February 1939.

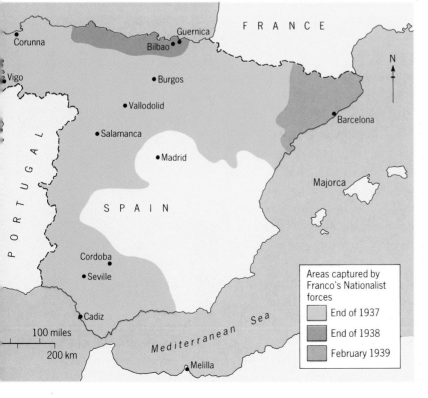

Franco

Francisco Franco (1892–1975) was a soldier and one of the main organizers of the 1936 revolt against the Republican government of Spain. In the Spanish Civil War which followed, Franco led the *Falange* (Fascist Party). With support from Hitler and Mussolini, he finally defeated the Republicans in 1939. His next move was to ban all political parties except *Falange*. Franco ruled Spain as a dictator. During the Second World War he was sympathetic to Hitler, but kept Spain neutral. In 1969 he nominated King Juan Carlos as his successor.

2.5 The Rhineland and Austria

Crowds cheer German soldiers as they enter the Rhineland, 7 March 1936.

B

SOURCE

The 48 hours after the march into the Rhineland were the most nerve-racking of my life.

Adolf Hitler, overheard talking to his generals soon after the event.

C

SOURCE

The German army was not strong enough for war; its officers had orders to retreat at once if the French began to fight. Hitler need not have worried. Some French generals were secretly fascist. Others were only prepared to defend French territory. They told their government that the French army was not fit to launch an attack.

L. Snellgrove, 'The Modern World Since 1870', 1981.

At the end of the First World War, as part of the Treaty of Versailles, Germany was forbidden to put troops or build fortresses within 30 miles of the Rhine. Germany was also forbidden to join with Austria to make one German-speaking country.

Hitler was determined to challenge these restrictions. By the mid-1930s he felt ready to do so. He had already begun to defy the controls placed on Germany by the Allies in 1919. He had introduced conscription and begun to build up the German armed forces. He had left the League of Nations. No one had stopped him from doing any of these things. He had also seen Japan take Manchuria and Italy take Abyssinia. The League of Nations had not stopped them either. He had seen the Stresa Front collapse almost as soon as it had been formed. By 1936 he was prepared to challenge the League of Nations again.

On 7 March 1936 German troops marched into the Rhineland unchallenged. The Germans who lived there greeted them enthusiastically. Although Germany was breaking the Treaty of Versailles, there were only mild protests from Britain and France. Many argued the Rhineland was German territory and Hitler could do what he liked with it.

D

SOURCE

Perhaps you will find me one morning in Vienna. The SA and the Legion [SS] will come in after the troops looking for revenge.

Hitler to the Austrian leader Von Schuschnigg, February 1938.

In 1936 Hitler and Mussolini formed an alliance called the **Rome–Berlin Axis**. Mussolini had been angered by attempts by the League to stop him taking over Abyssinia. Hitler wanted the Italians to support him in his plans for conquering more land in Europe.

Hitler's next aim was to create an *Anschluss* (union) with Austria. Austrian Nazis organized demonstrations and carried out terrorist attacks on the Austrian government. In February 1938 the Austrian leader **Von Schuschnigg** was invited to meet Hitler. He was ordered to make the Austrian Nazi Party legal, release Nazi terrorists in prison, invite Nazis to join his government, and have closer links with Germany.

When Von Schuschnigg returned to Vienna he decided to let the Austrian people vote on whether they agreed with these demands. He ordered a vote called a **plebiscite**. Hitler was furious; he feared the vote might go against him. He ordered Austrian Nazis to revolt and called on Mussolini for support.

Von Schuschnigg was forced to resign. He was replaced by a Nazi. On 12 March 1938 German troops crossed the frontier into Austria. One month later 99.75% of the Austrian electorate voted that they wanted the *Anschluss*.

Freud

Sigmund Freud (1856–1939) was an Austrian Jew who lived most of his life in Vienna. In 1938 he fled to London to avoid being persecuted by the Germans, who had occupied Austria. He died in 1939.

Freud is famous for being the founder of 'psychoanalysis'. This is a method of treating mentally disturbed people by encouraging them to reveal details of their lives which are hidden in their 'sub-conscious'. Freud believed that the experiences children have in childhood often affect their behaviour when they grow to adulthood. His most famous work, *The Interpretation of Dreams*, was published in 1900.

E

SOURCE

Austrians cheer German troops in Vienna, 14 March 1938.

2.6 Peace at Any Price?

In the 1930s the western democracies of Britain and France adopted a **policy of appeasement** towards Hitler and Mussolini. This means that they tried to negotiate and meet many of the demands of the dictators in order to avoid war. The Treaty of Versailles had set up the country of **Czechoslovakia** in eastern Europe. Two and a half million Germans lived in the western part of this country, in an area called the **Sudetenland**. After the Anschluss with Austria, German territory surrounded much of western Czechoslovakia. Hitler threatened that if the Sudeten Germans were not given the right to rule themselves (**self determination**) he would declare war on Czechoslovakia.

The British Prime Minister **Chamberlain** flew to Germany on 15 September 1938 to try to persuade Hitler not to fight. Hitler agreed to give the Czechs until 1 October to do as he demanded. Chamberlain put pressure on the Czech leader **Benes** to agree to give up those parts of the Sudetenland in which Germans made up the majority of the population. On 23 September Chamberlain met Hitler once more. The German leader refused to accept what Benes had offered. Instead he demanded that the Czechs give up *all* of the Sudetenland to Germany.

It looked as if war would follow. The Czechs were allies of the French and the USSR, and they had a well-organized small army. On 28 September Chamberlain was invited to meet with Hitler, Mussolini and the French leader Daladier in Munich, Germany. They would try to sort out the problem. The Czechs were not allowed to take part and the USSR was not invited. At this meeting it was agreed that Hitler could have all of the Sudetenland. The Czechs would have to accept the arrangement or fight Germany on their own. Hitler promised he would make no more demands in Europe. On 1 October Germany took the Sudetenland. That month Germany allowed Hungary and Poland to take land from the Czechs, too.

 A In war there are no winners but all are losers. It is these thoughts that made me feel it my duty to avoid a repeat of the Great War.

Chamberlain, September 26

 B I must confess to a distrust of the USSR. I have no belief in her ability to fight. And I distrust her motives.

Chamberlain, April 1939.

 C To go into battle without our Empire behind us – and we won't have it on this issue – is unthinkable.

Henderson, British Ambassador to Berlin, September 1938.

 D We must reduce the numbers of our potential enemies and gain the support of potential allies.

British military chiefs, 1937.

 E In 1938 Britain and France let Hitler have whatever they considered necessary for the peace of Europe. They felt that Hitler had certain definite aims and that once he had achieved these he would be satisfied.

S. Lee, 'Nazi Germany', 1989.

How Czechoslovakia was divided, 1938.

Legend:
- Given to Germany at Munich
- Seized by Poland, September
- Given to Hungary by Germany and Italy, October

Map labels: GERMANY, POLAND, Sudeten Germans, Silesia, Prague, Kracow, Teschen, CZECHOSLOVAKIA, Brno, Danube, Vienna, Bratislava, AUSTRIA, HUNGARY, Budapest, ROMANIA

miles 0 — 100
km 0 — 200

F Chamberlain decided that the demand for the return of the Sudetenland was reasonable. Here was another Versailles mistake which needed correcting.

L. Snellgrove, 'The Modern World Since 1870', 1968.

G It was a deliberate policy aimed at directing the violence eastward and against the USSR.

A later Soviet view of appeasement. From 'Recalling the Past', published by the Novosti Press Agency, Moscow, 1985.

Speech bubbles:
- Nothing to do with Britain
- British Empire won't help
- Germans treated badly after WWI
- Britain had o many possible enemies
- Hitler would soon stop making demands
- ritish army t ready for war
- Fear of Communist USSR
- Fear of war

Why did Chamberlain adopt a policy of appeasement?

Chamberlain

Neville Chamberlain (1869–1940) is famous as the British Prime Minister of the 1930s who tried to avoid war.

Chamberlain's Public Offices	
1905	Lord Mayor of Birmingham
1918	MP for Birmingham
1923	Minister for Health
1931	Chancellor of the Exchequer
1937	Prime Minister

Chamberlain believed that direct, one-to-one discussions with Hitler could avoid war. This policy was bitterly opposed by Winston Churchill, who believed that Chamberlain should take a more confrontational approach. Although Chamberlain reached agreement with Hitler at Munich in 1938, Hitler broke his promises. Chamberlain abandoned his policy of appeasement in 1939. After the invasion of Norway, Chamberlain resigned.

2.7 1939: The Collapse of Peace

In 1939 the peace in Europe was shattered and the Second World War began. The policy of appeasement had failed. Hitler had finally pushed the western democracies too far.

On 15 March 1939 Hitler broke his promise to the Czechs and seized the western parts of the country, called **Bohemia** and **Moravia**. Only the eastern part, called **Slovakia**, was left and it was a puppet state of the Germans. Hitler also allowed his friends the Hungarians to take a chunk of eastern Slovakia, called **Ruthenia**.

One week later Hitler seized the city of **Memel** from **Lithuania**, on the Polish borders. The British were shocked and promised that they would stand by the Poles if Germany attacked. The Germans wished to control the **'Polish Corridor'** which divided the bulk of Germany from the Germans of East Prussia and which gave Poland a route to the sea. Already Nazis were active in the city of **Danzig** (modern **Gdansk**) which was run by the League of Nations.

B SOURCE

By the occupation of Prague, Hitler put himself in the wrong and destroyed the German case against the Treaty of Versailles.

Henderson, ex-British Ambassador in Berlin, looking back in 1948.

C SOURCE

In the event of any action which clearly threatens Polish independence, His Majesty's government would feel bound to lend the Polish government all support in their power.

Chamberlain to the British House of Commons, 31 March 1939.

D SOURCE

There is no question of sparing Poland. We cannot expect a repetition of the Czech affair. There will be war. Our task is to isolate Poland.

Hitler to his generals, May 1939.

'Forced to salute the invading Nazis, Prague's population can only weep' – 'Chronicle of the 20th Century', 1988.

'German people welcoming the German army entering either the Sudetenland, or Austria' – Imperial War Musem, 1992.

A SOURCE

The final steps to war, 1939.

Germany by the end of 1938

Bohemia/Moravia seized by Germans, March 1939

Ruthenia – seized by Hungary, March 1939

Slovakia – dominated by Germans

Area invaded by USSR, Sept 1939

Invaded by Germans, September 1939

Molotov

Vyacheslav Molotov was a Soviet statesman who played an important role in relations between the USSR and the West between 1939 and 1956. He took part in the 1917 Bolshevic Revolution and was appointed to the Politbureau (inner council) in 1921. He became Chairman of the Council of Ministers in 1930 and Foreign Minister in 1939. He was largely responsible for the negotiations which brought about the Nazi–Soviet pact of 1939. During the war he advised Stalin on foreign policy, but his influence declined after Kruschev took power. He was ambassador to Mongolia from 1957 to 1960 and then retired from public life.

In April 1939 the Italians invaded **Albania**. The British then promised **Greece** and **Romania** that they would stand by them if they were attacked. The British leaders no longer trusted Hitler and his allies. They hoped that by finally standing up to him a war could still be avoided. On 18 April the USSR asked Britain and France to make an agreement that they would defend each other if attacked. The British leaders did not like the Communists and did not reply with any enthusiasm or speed.

Then the seemingly impossible happened. On 23 August Germany and the USSR signed an agreement promising not to attack one another. This was called the **Nazi–Soviet Pact**. A secret part of the pact was an agreement to share Poland's lands between the two countries. On 1 September Germany invaded Poland. On 3 September Britain and France declared war. They believed that this was the only way to stop the spread of German power.

3.1 War in Western Europe, 1939–41

On 1 September 1939 German troops moved into Poland. They used a new kind of warfare called **Blitzkrieg** (lightning war). First the enemy was 'softened up' by the German **Panzer** tank units and the *Luftwaffe* bombers, then the infantry moved in to mop up. Britain and France both declared war on Germany but could not offer any help to Poland. Stalin also invaded Poland from the east, as had been agreed in the Nazi–Soviet Pact. The Poles were defeated within four weeks.

The British expected Hitler's bombers at any moment. The government tried to prepare for this: gas masks were issued to all civilians; a system of air-raid warnings was set up; lights were blacked out; children from big cities were evacuated to the countryside; cinemas and theatres closed. But for months nothing happened. The lack of fighting led people to nickname this period the 'Phoney War', or more humorously 'Sitzkrieg'!

But in April 1940 war arrived in western Europe. Hitler's forces captured **Norway** and **Denmark**, despite attempts by the British and French to stop them. In May, Chamberlain resigned as Prime Minister and was replaced by **Winston Churchill**. A few days later Hitler launched his attack on France ('**Operation Yellow**'). Germany invaded the Netherlands, Belgium and Luxembourg, then marched on into France, avoiding the **Maginot line**, France's great line of fortifications along the German border. By 20 May German forces had reached the Channel coast.

'Operation Yellow' – the German invasion of France, May 1940.

A

SOURCE

A contemporary painting by Charles Cundall showing troops being rescued from the beaches of Dunkirk.

Date	Figures given by RAF in 1940	Figures given by RAF after war	Figures in German High Command Diary
15 August	185	76	55
18 August	155	71	49
15 September	185	56	50
27 September	153	55	42
Totals	678	258	196

The **British Expeditionary Force**, which had been sent to help the French, was forced to join them in retreat. Soon more than 300,000 Allied troops were penned in around the port of Dunkirk. Hitler ordered Goering, the Commander of the *Luftwaffe*, to use his bombers to destroy these forces.

Britain launched a desperate effort to rescue the soldiers. The government appealed for help to get them off the beaches. Between 24 May and 4 June an armada of hundreds of small, privately owned boats sailed to France and helped the Royal Navy to ferry nearly 330,000 French and English troops to larger ships offshore. The Dunkirk rescue has become one of the most famous events in British history. Even today great bravery in the face of overwhelming odds is often referred to as the 'Dunkirk spirit'.

Within a month of the Dunkirk evacuation France surrendered to Germany. Instead of occupying the whole of France, Germany allowed southern France to set up a government run by General Pétain at **Vichy**. The **Vichy Government** was really controlled by the Germans. However, it was run by the French themselves – Hitler hoped that this would stop the French colonies and navy from going over to the British side.

Britain braced itself for an invasion, but Hitler knew that before he could invade he would have to destroy the **Royal Air Force** (RAF). Between July and September 1940 the RAF and the German *Luftwaffe* fought the '**Battle of Britain**' in the skies over England. The British came perilously close to defeat, but managed to fight off the German attacks. On 17 September Hitler abandoned his planned invasion. Instead he decided to bomb Britain's cities. From autumn 1940 until spring 1941 wave after wave of German bombers attacked London and other main centres of population and industrial production. But like the Battle of Britain, Hitler's 'Blitz' proved unsuccessful. Britain continued to stand firm.

Numbers of German aircraft shot down on four days during the Battle of Britain in 1940.

Pétain

Henri-Philippe Pétain (1856–1951) was a French First World War hero, who was later sentenced to death for treason. He was educated at St Cyr military college and became a Colonel in 1912. After he won a famous victory against the Germans at Verdun in 1916 he was appointed Commander-in-Chief of the French forces on the Western Front. When the Germans occupied northern France in the Second World War, Pétain became head of the Vichy government, which ruled unoccupied France. But after the Germans overran Vichy in France in 1942, he became little more than a puppet ruler. At the end of the war he was condemned to death for treason, but his sentence was reduced to life imprisonment.

3.2 The German Invasion of the USSR

Despite the signing of the Nazi–Soviet Pact in 1939, Germany and the USSR remained bitter rivals. Hitler saw the Slav people of the USSR as **Untermenschen** (sub-humans) and detested Communism. He wanted to conquer the USSR and take control of its valuable oil fields and fertile wheat plains. A defeated USSR would also provide *Lebensraum* for German settlers. The Soviet people could then be put to work as slave labourers.

Hitler had planned to invade the USSR in spring 1941. But '**Operation Barbarossa**', as the Germans called the attack, did not actually take place until 22 June. Hitler had to spend the spring of that year rescuing his Italian ally, Mussolini, from the difficulties he had got into during his invasion of Greece. This delay proved to be vitally important.

When the invasion was finally launched the Germans soon drove deep into Soviet territory. Their Panzer tank units advanced up to 20 miles a day. By November the Germans were threatening Moscow, Leningrad and Kiev. What Hitler had not expected, however, was that his troops would still be fighting when winter came. The temperature in the USSR rarely rises above freezing point from late November to early April, and the Germans were totally unprepared for the severity of such weather. At the end of November their advance came to a halt as oil froze in the tanks. Equipped only with summer uniforms, more than 1,000,000 of the German troops suffered from frostbite. They were also short of supplies, as the retreating Soviets had adopted a '**scorched earth**' policy, destroying anything which they could not carry away.

As the Germans dug in for the winter, the better equipped Soviets launched a series of counter-offensives, led by Marshal Zhukov. They also moved over 1500 arms and munitions factories deep into the eastern USSR. There they would be safe from the Germans. By the end of 1942 these factories were pouring out weapons for the army. Help was coming from abroad, too, as Britain and later the USA sent tanks and aircraft.

A **SOURCE**

A German soldier using a flame-thrower during an attack on a Soviet village.

B **SOURCE**

Rifles became so cold that if a man picked his up with a bare hand, it stuck to the rifle. It was so cold that he didn't realize what had happened. So when he took his hand away, he found that the flesh of the palm and fingers remained on the rifle. It was the height of danger to urinate in the open; men were literally and permanently unmanned for being so rash.

The effects of the cold in the USSR. From R. Seth, 'Operation Barbarossa', 1964.

The Germans continued their advance when spring came. Their main aim was to capture the oilfields of the Caucasus region. But when they reached **Stalingrad** Hitler ordered his Sixth Army to take the city. This was to prove a mistake. The Soviets were prepared to stake everything to hold the city. They also proved more effective at the kind of street fighting that was involved in what became known as the **Battle of Stalingrad**.

In November fresh Soviet troops arrived and the Germans found themselves surrounded. Despite Hitler's orders that he should fight on, **Von Paulus**, the Commander of the Sixth Army, surrendered in February 1943. The remaining German forces began a long and miserable retreat towards home. The invasion of the USSR had proved to be a terrible mistake for Hitler. It had cost Germany nearly 200,000 men. But the USSR had suffered even greater losses. Nearly 20 million Soviet soldiers and civilians had died defending their homeland.

C

SOURCE

A Soviet cartoon from the Second World War showing Hitler ordering his troops to their death.

The German attack on the USSR, 1941–2.

N

→ German advance, June 1941 to December 1942

⊶ Furthest extent of German advances, December 1942

→ Soviet advances after 1942

0   300 miles
0   400 km

FINLAND

Baltic Sea

Leningrad – under siege 1941–4

• Moscow – German advance stopped Dec. 1941

Smolensk •

P O L A N D

• Kiev

Stalingrad – Germans defeated 1942–3

SLOVAKIA

HUNGARY

C A U C A S U S

R O M A N I A

Black Sea

Zhukov

Georgi Zhukov (1896–1974) was the USSR's leading Second World War general. After the First World War he became an expert on the use of tanks. In the Second World War Zhukov led the defence of Leningrad in 1941 and raised the German seige of Stalingrad in 1942. He commanded the Soviet forces which advanced into Germany and captured Berlin in May 1945. After the war he became Minister of Defence under Kruschev. He retired in 1957.

3.3 War in the Pacific

By the end of 1941 the Second World War had spread to the **Pacific**. As we saw in Unit 2.1, after 1929 Japan was facing economic difficulties which it believed could only be solved by winning new territory.

Following its invasion of Manchuria Japan began devising a plan for 'New Order' in Asia. It said that the time had come for the Europeans and Americans to be expelled and for the **Greater Asia Co-Prosperity Plan** to be put into operation. This involved setting up an organization under Japan's leadership to provide economic growth and political independence. In reality it meant Japan gaining control of Asia and exploiting its raw materials for Japan's own use.

Japan faced strong opposition from the Americans. The USA had been concerned about the growth of Japanese power ever since the First World War. It was not prepared to see Japan build an empire in South-East Asia and threaten US trade. So, in 1940, the USA imposed a total **embargo** (block) on the sale of oil to Japan. Since 80% of Japan's oil came from the USA, it would be just a matter of time before Japanese industries ground to a halt.

By 1941 the Japanese had come to the conclusion that they needed to take military action to seize control of the raw materials of Asia. Britain and Holland had colonies in Asia, but they were too busy fighting Germany to be able to protect their possessions in the East. What *would* be a problem for the Japanese was the power of the US Navy, which could prevent any Japanese take-over. The Japanese therefore decided on a surprise attack to destroy the US Pacific fleet at **Pearl Harbor**, Hawaii. Then they could take over South-East Asia before the Americans rebuilt their navy.

SOURCE A

A Dutch poster printed in England during the Second World War. It says, 'The Indies must be freed. Work and fight for it!' Before the war the East Indies were part of the Dutch Empire.

The attack came at 8 a.m. on Sunday 7 December 1941. Japanese aircraft swept down on the US base. They destroyed eight battleships and more than 350 planes. They also killed 2400 Americans. But they did not totally destroy the US fleet as they had hoped. Instead they 'awoke a sleeping giant'. The USA immediately declared war on Japan, and on Japan's allies, Germany and Italy. Within two years the Americans had rebuilt their fleet and gone on the attack against Japan. By that time, however, the Japanese had achieved their aim of winning control of much of South-East Asia.

On Christmas Day 1941 the Japanese captured the British base of **Hong Kong**. They took two US bases, **Guam** and **Wake**, before the year was over. Early in 1942 the Japanese marched through **Malaya** and in February captured the great British naval base at **Singapore**. This was to be Britain's worst defeat of the whole war, with 80,000 troops taken prisoner. In March 1942 the Japanese captured **Java**, followed rapidly by the rest of the **Dutch East Indies**. **Burma** (a British colony) fell in April and the **Philippines** (USA) in May. By July 1942 much of **New Guinea** had been captured and **Australia** was under threat from the Japanese.

Japan had set up its 'New Order' in South-East Asia, but could it defend it against the might of the USA?

The war in the Pacific, 1941–2.

B

SOURCE

The Allied soldiers found it very difficult to cope with jungle conditions. Unlike the rice-eating Japanese, they suffered through inadequate diet and fell victim to a variety of tropical diseases. The humidity and heat, combined with the problem of mosquitoes, meant that every day large numbers of men were unfit for combat.

Problems encountered by Allied soldiers fighting in the Pacific area. From N. Kelly, 'The Second World War', 1989.

MacArthur

Douglas MacArthur (1880–1964) attended the famous army college at West Point. He fought in the First World War and showed great skill as an officer. After the war he became Superintendent of West Point and in 1932 was sent to break up Washington's 'Hoovervilles' (shanty towns of homeless, unemployed people). He retired in 1937 but he was called out of retirement to try to stop the Japanese occupation of the Philippines. He led the campaign against the Japanese and received their surrender in September 1945. MacArthur commanded the UN troops in the Korean War until he was sacked by President Truman in 1951.

3.4 The Allied Victories in the West

At the beginning of 1941, Hitler's Germany seemed in a very strong position. Only Britain stood between Hitler and victory. But by 1942 the situation had changed dramatically. In June 1941 Hitler launched his ill-fated attack on the USSR, and in December the USA entered the war. By 1945 the Allies were so strong that Germany's defeat was unavoidable.

The North African Front

In Africa, Britain was fighting Italian and German forces for control of the Mediterranean coast and the Suez Canal. The British defeated the Italians, but found the German forces under **Field Marshal Rommel** much harder to beat. However, a new British commander, **General Montgomery**, led the British to a decisive victory at **El Alamein** in October 1942. When US forces arrived to help in November 1942, the Allies began to push the Italians and Germans out of Africa. Then, in July 1943, they invaded Sicily and began to march through Italy towards Germany.

The Soviet Front

After their defeat at Stalingrad in 1942, the Germans suffered further defeats in 1943 and 1944. Their glorious campaign became a desperate retreat. By July 1944 the Soviet forces had pushed them back into Poland. By April 1945 they had liberated eastern Europe from German control. In May they reached Berlin.

The Western Front

By 1944 the Allies were ready to launch an attack on Hitler in Europe. On 6 June – D-Day – Allied forces under the command of the US General Eisenhower landed on five beaches in Normandy. By the end of that day they had managed to establish themselves, and supplies and reinforcements began arriving from across the English Channel. Then the Allies began advancing across France. By September northern France, Luxembourg and Belgium had been liberated. General de Gaulle, who had established himself as leader of the 'Free French' while in exile in London, returned to Paris to head the government.

A **SOURCE**

In many German cities people were camping among the ruins of their former homes without light, heat or water and were forced to scavenge like animals.

S. L. Case, 'The Second World War', 1981.

B **SOURCE**

ВПЕРЕД, НА ЗАПАД!

A Second World War poster encouraging Soviet forces to victory over the Germans.

Meanwhile the Allies pressed on. They overcame a German counter attack in December 1944 (the **Battle of the Bulge**) and reached Berlin in April 1945.

The bombing campaign

From 1942 the Allies launched a series of **bombing raids** on Germany. Sir Arthur ('Bomber') Harris organized 'thousand bomber' raids which caused havoc in German cities and destroyed industrial sites. In one raid alone, at Dresden in February 1945, 135,000 Germans died. By April 1945 much of Berlin had been turned to rubble and its people were starving.

By the end of April 1945 Germany was on the point of collapse. On 30 April Hitler and his wife, Eva Braun, committed suicide in his bunker under Berlin. Admiral Doenitz assumed command and surrendered to the Allies on 7 May.

Montgomery

Field Marshall Bernard Law Montgomery (1887–1976) was the British soldier sent to Africa to command the Eighth Army in 1942. He won a spectacular victory over the German forces led by Field Marshall Rommel at El Alamein which led to British control of North Africa. Montgomery was one of the commanders of the Allied forces during the D-Day landings and the drive through France and into Germany.

The defeat of Germany.

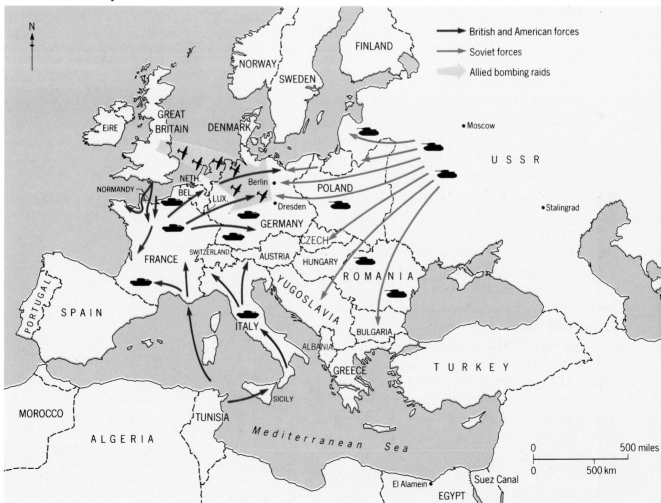

3.5 Victory in the Pacific

By late 1942 the Japanese had captured much of South-East Asia, but there were signs that the tide was already beginning to turn. In the spring of 1942 the US Navy won victories at **Coral Sea** and **Midway Island**. The US fleet now dominated the Pacific Ocean.

American forces then began the process of recapturing Japan's conquests. Their plan of attack was based on 'island-hopping'. The aim was to leap-frog across the Pacific, island by island, until they reached Japan. Their first reconquest was **Guadalcanal** in August 1942. But it cost more than 1600 US lives. The Americans discovered that the Japanese were fanatical fighters. They considered surrender to be dishonourable and believed that soldiers should fight to the death. This made them very difficult to defeat, even when they were faced with heavy losses. For example, 24,000 Japanese soldiers were killed defending Guadalcanal.

During 1943 and 1944 the Americans managed to recapture one Pacific island after another, often inflicting heavy losses on the Japanese. In June 1944 the Japanese lost 480 planes and three aircraft carriers at the **Battle of the Philippine Sea**. Almost 170,000 Japanese soldiers died when the Americans re-captured the Philippines. In June the Americans took **Okinawa**, an island just 400 miles to the south of Japan.

A SOURCE

Bear in mind the fact that to be captured is a disgrace to the Army. Also your parents and family will never be able to hold up their heads again. Always save the last bullet for yourself.

Extract from the Japanese Army Manual issued during the war.

B

'My God, what have we done?'

Captain R. Lewis, co-pilot of the Enola Gay on seeing the effects of the bomb.

C

'This is the greatest thing in history.'

US President Truman, on being told of the dropping of the bomb.

D SOURCE

The city of Hiroshima after the dropping of the atomic bomb.

The Japanese were so determined not to give in that they were literally prepared to commit suicide. **Kamikaze** or suicide pilots would volunteer for missions in which they became 'living bombs'. The pilot would take off in an obsolete plane, packed with explosives, then fly directly at a US warship. When the US forces attacked Okinawa, some 2000 Kamikaze pilots died, sinking 30 US warships.

By mid-1945 the Japanese were in a desperate position. Since 1944 US bombers had flown unchallenged over Japan. They dropped many incendiary bombs which caused dreadful destruction to Japanese cities. On 15 March 80,000 Japanese died in a bombing raid on the city of Tokyo. This was more people than had been killed in the whole of England during the Blitz. Japan had also been cut off from its supplies of raw materials, and a US blockade was resulting in widespread food shortages. In Burma, Japanese forces were also being defeated by the British.

By the end of July 1945, the Japanese government asked the USSR to approach the US government to see if terms for surrender could be agreed. However, US President Truman was convinced that Japan's surrender must be unconditional. So the Japanese forces continued to fight. Truman was faced with the problem of how to defeat the Japanese without the enormous loss of US life that an invasion would bring.

The answer seemed to lie in the new weapon that US scientists had developed. This was the **atomic bomb**. Tests had shown that it was capable of destroying whole cities. If one of these bombs were to be dropped on a Japanese city, it would surely cause them to surrender. Truman sent the Japanese an ultimatum demanding unconditional surrender. The Japanese ignored the ultimatum.

At 8.15 a.m. on 6 August 1945 the US bomber *Enola Gay* flew over the city of **Hiroshima**. Colonel Tibbets released the bomb. The massive explosion destroyed the city. Over 80,000 civilians died from the explosion – many more died later from the effects of radiation. Incredibly, the Japanese still did not surrender. On 9 August a further bomb was dropped on **Nagasaki**, killing 40,000 Japanese. On the same day the USSR invaded Japanese-held Manchuria. Now the Japanese had no choice. Emperor Hirohito broadcast the news of Japan's surrender on 15 August 1945. The war was over.

E

SOURCE

My daughter had no burns and only minor external wounds. However, on 4 September she suddenly became sick. She had spots all over her body. Her hair began to fall out. She vomited small clumps of blood many times. After ten days of agony she died.

A Hiroshima father's account of his daughter's death.

Einstein

Albert Einstein (1879–1955) was a German Jew who fled Germany to avoid persecution. He was born at Ulm in Germany and moved to Switzerland at the age of 15. While working in Basle in 1905 he began to develop his Theory of Relativity, which is the basis of atomic power. After a time as Professor in Zurich and Prague, Einstein returned to Germany and in 1921 won the Nobel Prize for Physics.

In 1933 he fled to the USA to avoid Nazi persecution. He became worried that his work could be used to develop an atomic bomb. In 1939 he warned President Roosevelt of the danger to world peace if Nazi Germany developed such a bomb. He was so concerned that he tried unsuccessfully to have the United Nations take control of atomic energy.

4.1 Life in Nazi Europe

By the end of 1942 Nazi Germany controlled almost all of Europe and was opposed only by the USSR and Britain. All other European countries were either neutral or allied to Germany. The Nazis exploited the lands they controlled for their own use. Local resources, such as Polish coal, were used in the German war effort. Many factories were taken over and put to work making goods for Germany. Some were simply closed down and their valuable machinery shipped home to be used in German factories. Food, too, was taken from conquered countries and transported to German soldiers and civilians. The Nazis were not concerned if this caused starvation to the population of the country from which the food was taken.

Perhaps the major resource exploited by the Germans was **labour**. To produce the food and goods needed to win the war Germany had to find millions of extra workers for its farms and factories. The answer was to use slave labour. By 1944 there were more than seven million slave workers in Germany. About half of these were from the USSR. The Germans treated prisoners of war from western Europe well, since most of them were **Aryans**, like the Germans (see Unit 4.3). Those from eastern Europe were generally **Slavs**, people whom Hitler saw as sub-human and not worthy of respect. Germany took more than five million Soviet soldiers prisoner during the war. Many were transported to Germany as slave labour.

A **SOURCE**

Of 3,600,000 Soviet prisoners, only a few hundred thousand are still able to work fully. Camp commanders have forbidden food to be put at their disposal, instead they have let them starve to death. Even on the way to the work camps civilians were not allowed to give the prisoners food. If prisoners could not keep up, they were shot before the eyes of horrified civilians.

Letter from the Nazi minister in charge of the German-occupied USSR, February 1942.

Europe at the end of 1942.

Not everything that the Nazis took was to help them win the war. As they occupied land, they took many of the most valuable paintings, sculptures and other art treasures. Many of these found their way back to Germany. Goering, in particular, amassed a valuable collection of stolen art treasures.

The harshness of German rule varied according to the status of the conquered countries. In the west the Germans took control using local politicians if possible. In Norway Major Quisling took charge. In France General Pétain headed the Vichy Government. But the Germans always made sure their rule was obeyed. Anyone who opposed the Nazis was dealt with either by the **Gestapo** (the secret police) or the **SS** (an organization of 'elite' troops which was used to control opposition to Hitler). The SS was also responsible for running the concentration camps.

In eastern Europe, however, the Nazis planned to clear the population to make *Lebensraum* for German settlers. Jews were transported to the death camps (see Unit 4.3); millions of other eastern Europeans were sent to work as slave labour in Germany. In the USSR special 'action groups' followed behind the German army. Their target was to kill civilians and prisoners-of-war in territory won by the Nazis. Over a million people died in this way. It was little wonder that Soviet soldiers sometimes treated German civilians with brutality when they advanced into Nazi Germany.

Goering

Hermann Goering (1893–1946) joined the Nazi Party shortly after its foundation and was wounded in the Munich *Putsch* of 1923. Hitler appointed him Air Minister in 1933. In 1936 he began to prepare Germany's air force for war. In 1940 Hitler gave him the special title of 'Reichsmarshall'. He began to lose influence after Germany's failure to defeat Britain. He is said to have amassed a private fortune from war booty and to have been a drug addict. He was found guilty of war crimes at the Nuremberg trials and committed suicide.

German soldiers hanging Soviet citizens.

4.2 Opposition to the Nazis

Opposition within Germany

At the outbreak of war Hitler was popular in Germany. He had brought prosperity to Germany and re-occupied the lands taken in the hated Versailles Treaty. Most people were quite prepared to accept the restrictions that Nazi rule brought. They did not like the banning of opposition political parties and trade unions, or the persecution of the Jews, but this seemed an acceptable price to pay for Hitler's brilliant successes in foreign policy. Goebbel's clever use of **propaganda** (see Unit 4.7) also helped persuade Germans that all was well.

There were some people whose conscience refused to allow them to support what Hitler was doing. Some of these people would not join the army; others spoke out against Nazi policies. Such behaviour led to arrest and often execution. By 1939 Hitler had crushed most of the opposition, but there were still some Germans who were prepared to work to overthrow him. If caught, these people were shown no mercy. In 1944 a group of army leaders decided that Hitler was leading Germany to defeat. They tried to assassinate him, but their bomb plot failed. They were tortured and then hanged with piano wire.

Resistance movements

In countries occupied by Germany there were groups of people who were prepared to carry on an **underground war** against the Nazis. These were members of the **Resistance**. They played an important role in undermining the German war effort by sabotaging railways, bridges and factories. They kept up people's morale by secretly producing pamphlets and newspapers urging their countrymen and women to carry on the fight.

Although resistance groups existed in all occupied countries, the most famous is the French **Maquis**. It helped to organize escape routes for Allied airmen who had been shot down, carried out bombings of factories and disrupted German communications during the D-Day landings.

A **SOURCE**

Dear Parents: I must give you bad news – I have been condemned to death. Gustav and I did not sign up for the SS and so they condemned us to death. Both of us would rather die than stain our consciences with such deeds of horror. I know what the SS have to do.

Letter home from an imprisoned German agricultural worker.

B **SOURCE**

First they came for the Jews

– and I did not speak out -

because I was not a Jew

Then they came for the communists

– and I did not speak out -

because I was not a communist

Then they came for trade unionists

– and I did not speak out -

because I was not a trade unionist

Then they came for me -

and there was no one left

to speak out for me

A poem written by the German churchman, Pastor Niemoller, during his imprisonment by the Nazis.

SOURCE C

How to take a photograph in secret. The woman apparently fumbling in her bag, has a hidden camera (the lens can be seen just below the centre of the two rings).

SOURCE D

Within weeks of being put in charge, Heydrich arrested nearly 5000 Czech resistance workers. Most of them were executed. Yet this did not stop the sabotage. According to German sources, war production in Czech factories went down by 33%. Heydrich said that he had not done his job properly.

Dr. J-L Charles, 'Europe's Secret Armies', 1966.

In Czechoslovakia the Resistance assassinated the SS General Reynhard Heydrich. Nazi retaliation was severe. In the Czech village of Lidice all 192 males were shot, 82 children sent to the gas chambers, 35 older women sent to Auschwitz death camp (see Unit 4.3) and the remaining women put in a labour camp. Even the dogs were shot in their kennels. Then Lidice was burned to the ground.

At first Britain did not provide much help to the resistance groups. But the British soon realized how valuable these groups were not only for undermining the German war effort, but also for providing vital information for the Allies. Therefore in 1940 the British formed the **Special Operations Executive** to co-ordinate the work of the various resistance groups. SOE agents were smuggled into occupied areas to give support to the local fighters.

Heydrich

Reinhard Heydrich (1904–42) was Hitler's number two during the Second World War. Unlike most of the other leaders, he resembled the 'Aryan' perfection which Hitler wanted, having blonde hair and blue eyes.

Heydrich was made head of the Gestapo in 1936. In 1941 he took charge of the policy of transporting Jews from all parts of Europe to the concentration camps for extermination. Some historians believe that he could have been Hitler's successor, but in 1942 he was assassinated by Czech partisans.

4.3 The Holocaust

Throughout history the **Jews** have been persecuted. They were often expelled from countries in the Middle Ages and have been victims of racial attacks in many countries during the 20th century. Yet despite thousands of years of persecution, the Jews have never experienced such dreadful treatment as they received at the hands of Hitler's Nazis.

In 1920 Adolf Hitler set out the views of the new Nazi Party. The people of Germany and northern Europe were members of the same 'Aryan' race. He believed that this race was the 'master race' born to rule over all the other races. The Jews, on the other hand, were an inferior people who polluted the pure Aryan race. Worse than this, the Nazis claimed that the Jews had intrigued with the Communists at the end of the First World War and in some unexplained way were responsible for Germany's defeat. Since the war, the Nazis said, the Jews had continued to work to undermine the German government. They were to blame for nearly all that was wrong with Germany.

At first people took little notice of Hitler's extreme views. After all, many Jews had fought with great bravery in the German armed forces in the war. Yet slowly but surely the Nazis began to win support. In January 1933 Hitler became Chancellor (leader of the German government). Now he had a chance to put his anti-Jewish ideas into practice.

The Nazis used school education to spread their anti-Jewish views. Children were taught to be proud to be Aryans and not to mix with Jews. Pupils even had lessons on how their own race was superior to all others. Jewish children were often ridiculed in front of their classmates.

The worst treatment, however, was given to adults. It began with people attacking Jewish shops or simply refusing to buy things from them. Sometimes Nazi soldiers stood outside to prevent people entering. In April 1933 all Jews working in the German civil service were thrown out of their jobs.

A SOURCE

A Nazi poster: 'We peasants are clearing out the muck'. The 'muck' shown is a group of Communists and Jews.

B 9.40–10.25 : Monday to Saturday: either Race Study or Ideology.

Extract from a German school timetable during the Nazi period.

C When I went to school at the age of 10, a third of my classmates were Jewish girls. I got on well with them, just as well as with all the others. From the older generation we learned that the Jews were wicked and that they would help Germany's enemies if there were a war.

 SOURCE

Memories of a German woman who was a schoolgirl in the Nazi period.

In 1935 local authorities banned Jews from swimming baths, parks and playing fields. They were also deprived of their right to vote. In the same year the **Nuremburg Laws** banned marriage between Jews and non-Jews. It also became illegal for Jews and non-Jews who weren't married to have sexual intercourse.

From 1938 the persecution of Jews was stepped up. When a German diplomat was murdered by a Jew in Paris, the Nazis carried out revenge attacks on German Jews. On 9 November 1938, over 7000 Jewish shops were attacked and synagogues and homes burned down. More than 30,000 Jews were rounded up and sent to concentration camps. This night has since been labelled *Kristallnacht* (Crystal Night). One leading Nazi complained about the cost to insurance companies. He said, 'they should have killed more Jews and broken less glass.'

Kristallnacht was the final straw for many Jews. Those who could get away joined the stream of Jews fleeing from Germany. For those who were unable to leave, a terrible fate was in store.

From T. Howarth 'The World Since 1900', 1979.

Eichmann

Karl Adolf Eichmann (1906–62) was born in Austria. He joined the German Nazi Party and became a member of the SS. From 1939 he was the Chief of the Gestapo's Jewish section, a post he particularly enjoyed as he was a well-known anti-Semite. He was a strong supporter of the policy of using gas chambers to kill Jews.

At the end of the war he was captured by US forces, but managed to keep his identity secret. He escaped from prison in 1945 and reached Argentina, where a number of other Nazi leaders were in hiding. In 1950 he was kidnapped by Israeli agents and taken back to Israel to face charges of 'crimes against humanity'. He was found guilty and executed.

D **SOURCE**

A cartoon showing anti-Jewish studies at school. The students are being taught to recognize Jewish 'characteristics'.

By the end of 1941 the Nazis had taken control of much of Europe. During this time they had conquered lands where millions of Jews lived. Many of these Jews were herded into **ghettoes** in the cities where they lived in such appalling conditions that starvation was common. Others were sent to **concentration camps** where they were put to work beside other 'undesirables' such as pacifists, communists, gypsies and homosexuals.

In 1941 Hitler devised his **Final Solution** to the Jewish 'problem'. A series of death camps was to be set up to carry out a mass slaughter of the whole Jewish population of Europe. During the next four years the Nazis were responsible for the deaths of over six million Jews in what has become known as the **Holocaust**.

Various methods were used to kill the Jews. Special death camps were set up to carry out the task. Sometimes the Jews were lined up alongside huge graves and shot so that they fell in. But as so many were to be killed, the Germans had to find more efficient ways of extermination. The method they chose was Cyclon B poison gas crystals. As many as 2000 people could be killed at one time. The victims were led into huge chambers, which were then sealed. The gas was released and after about three minutes everyone was dead. Then the bodies were taken away and burned. Useful by-products, like gold teeth, glasses and hair were kept for use by the Nazis. Other concentration camp inmates were used for medical experiments carried out without anaesthetic. This usually resulted in the death of the patient.

F SOURCE

The Führer has ordered the Jewish question to be settled once and for all. The Jews are sworn enemies of the German people and must be eradicated. Every Jew that we can lay our hands on is to be destroyed now, during the war, without exception.

An account from the memoirs of Rudolf Hess, Commandant of Auschwitz, telling how he was ordered to begin the extermination of the Jews.

G SOURCE

Then the prisoner guards had to find the small children who had been hidden. They opened the doors of the gas chamber and threw all the children in. 'Oh!' I said, 'I've never seen anything like it in my life. It's absolutely terrible.' My guide said, 'You get used to anything after a while.'

An SS officer's reaction on first witnessing the gassing of the Jews, recalled in a television interview in the 1960s.

The main concentration camps.

The Germans issued propaganda films showing good conditions in the camps. This encouraged many people to believe that reports of atrocities were exaggerated. After the liberation of the territory around camps such as **Auschwitz**, **Maidenek** and **Chelmno**, Britain and France could no longer pretend that they didn't know what was happening.

So far three million have died. It is the greatest mass-killing in recorded history: and it goes on daily, hourly, as regularly as the ticking of your watch. I have been lecturing Allied troops for three years now and their attitude is always the same. They don't believe it.

Arthur Koestler, an American journalist, writing in the 'New York Times' in January 1944.

Rows of corpses awaiting burial at one of the Nazi death camps.

Himmler

Heinrich Himmler (1900–45) was one of the most ruthless Nazi leaders. His career was a series of successes. In 1927 he became the deputy leader of the SS. He took over as leader in 1929 and later, in 1936, he became commander of the entire Nazi police force. His final promotion came in 1943 when he was made Minister of the Interior. Himmler set up the death camps for exterminating the Jews and, as head of the SS, he was responsible for carrying out the policy. He did so with a ruthless determination which made him a hated figure.

After the defeat of Germany he tried to escape in disguise but he was spotted and arrested by the British on 21 May 1945. He was not tried as a war criminal because, two days after his capture, he committed suicide.

4.4 The Home Front

The war brought great changes for Britain's civilian population. During the war German bombing caused extensive damage to housing and other public buildings (see Unit 4.6). Many parents worried about having their children looked after by strangers when they were evacuated to the countryside (see Unit 4.5). But there were also other important changes in people's life-style.

Working women

One of the major changes affected women. During the war many women went out to work for the first time. In 1939 more than a million people had been unemployed. When war broke out, however, all men aged 18–41 were called up to do military service and so there was a shortage of labour. The government looked to women to fill the gap. In 1941 women under 50 (except those with young families) had to register for war work. Some took jobs in factories. Others joined the Women's Land Army and worked on farms. By 1943 three-quarters of single women or those with children over 14 were doing war work. For many women the war brought their first taste of independence. They had their own wage packets and were responsible for the household finances. This was a significant step towards creating a more equal society. Some women also volunteered to work as nurses, or as members of the Women's Voluntary Service – their work included running canteens in bombed-out areas and sending food parcels to the troops.

A **SOURCE**

The word 'mock' crept into the vocabulary. There was mock cream, mock hamburgers, mock potato omelette – with plenty of potato, but no eggs. Mock duck was a recipe of beans, lentils, and mashed potatoes, flavoured with sage and onion and 'shaped to look like a duck'.

Margaret Costa, 'The Food Front', in the 'Sunday Times', 1965.

B **SOURCE**

Most people are better fed than they used to be. There are less fat people. For instance, with the adult milk ration of three pints a week, the amount of milk being drunk has actually increased since the war started.

The author George Orwell commenting during the Second World War on the effects of rationing.

C **SOURCE**

A wartime painting showing a woman working as a skilled machinist.

Men who were not fit enough for military service or who were in **reserved occupations** (jobs such as coal mining which were vital for the war effort) could still play a part as a volunteer. In the Blitz many volunteers acted as fire-fighters, ambulance drivers and air-raid wardens. Some joined the **Home Guard** (now affectionately known as Dad's Army) which was a volunteer reserve army, in case of invasion.

Rationing

During the war, German submarines sank ships bringing food to Britain. This caused food shortages. On 8 January 1940 the government tried to ensure that food supplies were shared out fairly by introducing **rationing**. Families were issued with a **ration book** which allowed them to buy a weekly amount of rationed food. At first only bacon, ham, butter and sugar were rationed; soon almost all basic foodstuffs were on ration.

Although people with money could always get food on the **black market**, most people tried to 'make do'. There were some very clever ways to prepare dishes that looked like the real thing – like wedding cakes, where most of what was under the icing was cardboard! The government encouraged people to grow more food. It used slogans like '**Dig for Victory**' and characters such as '**Potato Pete**' and '**Dr Carrot**' appeared on posters.

Fear

Perhaps the hardest aspect of the Home Front was the non-stop worry. Many parents were separated from their children, and wives from husbands. There was the constant fear of hearing that a loved one had died in battle or was the victim of a German bombing raid. It was with these terrible worries always at the back of their minds that the civilian population tried to cope with the day-to-day problems of being at war.

Wartime women on a protest march, 1942.

Orwell

George Orwell (1903–50) (whose real name was Eric Blair) was an English writer who was born in Bengal in India and educated at Eton. He returned to India after completing his schooling and served for five years with the Indian Imperial Police in Burma from 1922 to 1927. He then returned to Europe and began writing under the name of George Orwell.

He fought in the Spanish Civil War on the side of the Republicans and was seriously wounded. During the Second World War he was war correspondent for the BBC and the *Observer* newspaper. Many of his books reflect his support for the idea of Socialism. However, Orwell was bitterly critical of the USSR and wrote *Animal Farm* as a satire about Stalin's government. Orwell's most famous work, *1984*, was published in 1949. The book expresses his vision of a future where the government controls all aspects of human life.

4.5 Evacuees

Even before war broke out, the British government had made plans to evacuate children from major cities to the safety of the countryside. It was widely expected that within days of the declaration of war German bombers would attack British cities. No one wanted children to be put at risk. Some parents took up the government's offer of sending their children to the USA, but this practice soon came to an end once German submarines began sinking passenger ships.

At the end of August 1939 the government began moving nearly two million children out of the danger areas. When the bombs didn't come many of the evacuees returned home. However, there had to be further evacuation in October 1940 at the start of the Blitz.

Often the bewildered evacuees had little idea what was happening to them. Parents did not always know where their children were going. The government told the parents that their children would be well looked after, and the worrying parents had to hope this was true.

The evacuation process was often a great shock to all concerned. The vast majority of children were from poor areas of the big cities. The country families who received them were sometimes shocked by just how deprived many of these children were. For some evacuees their time in the countryside was a pleasurable experience. For others it was a time of great unhappiness.

B SOURCE

A government poster from the Second World War.

A SOURCE

The government has made plans for the removal of schoolchildren from what are called 'evacuable' areas to safer places. Householders have offered homes where the children will be made welcome. The children will have their schoolteachers and other helpers with them. The transport of three million children is an enormous undertaking. It would not be possible to let all parents know in advance the place to where each child will be sent. Of course it means heartache to be separated from your children, but you can be quite sure that they will be well looked after.

From a government leaflet, 'Evacuation: Why and How?', 1939.

C SOURCE

Everything was so clean in the room. We were given face flannels and tooth brushes. We'd never cleaned our teeth until then. And hot water from a tap. And there was a lavatory upstairs. And carpets. And something called an eiderdown. And clean sheets. This was all very odd. I didn't like it. It was scary.

Memories of a Second World War evacuee.

D

SOURCE

The woman said, 'Here's your meal' and gave us a tin of pilchards between the two of us and some bread and water. Now we'd been in a rich woman's house before, so we said, 'Where's the butter?' And we got a sudden wallop round the head. What we later found out was that the woman hated kids and was doing it for the extra money. So the meals were the cheapest you could dish up.

Michael Caine, who later became a famous actor, remembers life as an evacuee.

E

SOURCE

Children on their way to the countryside, 1938.

F

SOURCE

I thought it was a Sunday school outing down to the sea-side. And I looked out of the bus window and I saw my mother crying outside. I said to my brother, 'What's mummy crying for?' and my brother said, 'Shut up!'

Memories of a Second World War evacuee.

Michael Caine

Although Michael Caine (1933–) is one of the most famous of Britain's living actors, he does not come from a wealthy family. He was born in the East End of London (his real name is Maurice Micklewhite). Shortly after the war broke out he was evacuated to the safety of the countryside. He was educated at Wilson's Grammar School in Peckham, London, and served in the army in Berlin and in Korea between 1951 and 1953. After his army service he worked in repertory theatres in Horsham and Lowestoft and spent years as a struggling actor, playing minor parts in theatre and television.

In 1963 he played the part of an officer in the film *Zulu*. His performance in that part launched a career that has taken in hundreds of films and plays. He has been nominated four times for an Academy Award and in 1986 won an Oscar for Best Supporting Actor in *Hannah and Her Sisters*.

4.6 The Blitz

In September 1940 Hitler postponed his planned invasion of Britain. But while he might not be able to invade, he could still bomb. If he could cause sufficient terror in Britain's cities, then perhaps the British people would call upon Prime Minister Churchill to accept defeat. So Hitler ordered the *Luftwaffe* to launch a series of bombing raids on Britain's major cities.

The raids began on 7 September. London was bombed on 75 of the next 76 days. Perhaps the worst single raid on a British city came on 14 November 1940. Coventry suffered a ten-hour bombardment which destroyed one-third of the city and killed more than 4000 civilians. The Blitz continued until early summer 1941. Over 40,000 civilians were killed and more than two million people made homeless.

The government took a number of steps to try to protect civilians. It ordered a total **blackout**. All windows had to be covered by thick blackout curtains. Street and vehicle lights were shielded or dimmed. It was an offence to 'show a light' that might guide a German bomber to its target. Everyone was issued with a gas mask, in case the Germans dropped gas bombs. Windows were taped up to avoid flying splinters. Important buildings were protected by sandbags. Some people erected Anderson bomb shelters in their gardens, or used Morrison shelters indoors. In towns, there were public shelters where people could go if the air-raid warning sounded. In London, some families decided that the safest place to spend the night was on the platforms of the London Underground.

Despite the terrible bombardment, the British people did not give up. In fact they seemed to become more determined than ever to defeat the Germans.

A SOURCE

How much sleep did you get last night?

None	Less than 4 hours	4–6 hours	More than 6 hours
31%	32%	22%	15%

Results of a survey carried out in London on 12 September 1940.

A bus in a bomb crater caused by a raid in the Balham area of London, 1940.

Of course the press versions of life going on normally in the East End of London on Monday are horribly distorted. There was no bread, no electricity, no milk, no gas, no telephones. There was, therefore, every excuse for the people to be distressed.

An extract from a report by 'Mass Observation' in September 1940. This organization was a group of volunteers set up in 1937 to study all aspects of how British people lived and behaved.

The centre of Canterbury after heavy bombing.

Sir Arthur Harris

'Bomber' Harris (1892–1984) was born in Cheltenham, Gloucestershire and emigrated to Zimbabwe at the age of 10. During the First World War he fought the Germans in south-west Africa as a member of the 1st Rhodesian Regiment and later joned the Royal Flying Corps operating on the Western Front in France. He became a squadron leader in the newly formed RAF in 1918 and was promoted to Air Commodore in 1937. During the Second World War he became Deputy Chief of Air. This gave him the opportunity to put into operation his beliefs that the war could be more easily won by bombing enemy cities. In January 1943 he was given orders to disrupt German industry by a bombing campaign. Any German city with a population of over 100,000 inhabitants was considered to be a fair target. The bombing raids caused terrible destruction. On 13 February 1945 there were 135,000 casualties after a raid on Dresden in Germany. In 1992 a statue was erected in London in honour of the role played by Harris in helping Britain win the war.

4.7 Propaganda

Propaganda is the art of presenting information to influence the way people think. The Nazi Party made excellent use of propaganda during the 1930s in Germany. They set up a Ministry of Enlightenment and Propaganda headed by Joseph Goebbels. It proved highly effective in portraying the Nazi Party as the saviours of Germany.

During the Second World War both the Allies and the Axis powers (Germany, Italy and Japan) used propaganda to keep up the morale of the people. Sometimes this propaganda was blatant, showing the enemy as evil or wicked. Sometimes it was much more subtle. Newspapers could be encouraged (or instructed) to carry stories that seemed simply factual, but contained a hidden message. Modern party political broadcasts use the same approach nowadays to win support for political parties.

A **SOURCE**

A 1938 Nazi poster of Hitler. It reads, 'One people, one empire, one leader.'

Although there was no television during the war, both sides made films for cinema which were designed to show them in a good light. They also used radio stations to broadcast to the enemy. Not only were there official stations, such as the BBC and Radio Moscow, there were also some which were not what they appeared to be. Germany ran radio stations from within its borders that pretended to be French. Britain set up organizations which said that they were official German forces broadcasting stations. Both were used for propaganda purposes.

B During a war, news must be carefully controlled. Some news should not be made public. Every piece of news must be used to a purpose.

Extract from the diaries of Joseph Goebbels.

C The parades, processions, demonstrations, ceremonies and rallies by which the Nazis impressed the German people were nearly all his idea. He shared Hitler's belief that if you tell a lie often enough it will be believed.

SOURCE

Description of Goebbels from C. Culpin, 'Making History', 1984.

BOMB CRASHES DOWN HOSPITAL STAIRS

Daily Express Raid Reporters

One of the oldest London hospitals was hit by a bomb last night. The bomb fell down the main staircase and shattered it – but none of the patients in the wards leading off the stairs was injured.

Only one person was injured – a member of the medical staff who was in a small room at the top of the building.

A volunteer fireman climbed a ladder and brought him down from the wreckage.

Ward sisters and doctors opened the doors after the explosion and found a hole in front of them where the staircase had been.

They at once organised a human chain to carry the patients down a fire escape to beds on the ground floor.

A member of the hospital staff said shortly afterwards: "The doctor who was injured is undergoing an operation. His condition is fair.

"Everything is under control, and we are still recieving patients.

"We had to turn off the water and gas, but we have a little in our tanks, and we can still deal with urgent cases."

This is the fifth hospital in London damaged by Nazi bombs. One has been attacked twice.

Last night the raiders appeared to fly over London two or three at a time at frequent intervals. They dropped bombs indiscriminately over a wide area

Extract from the 'Daily Express', 16 September 1940.

SOURCE

E

We had become so accustomed to the explosive headlines, that we failed to grasp the full significance of the horror stories as they progressed from some humble position on the back page of the newspaper to blazing two-inch headlines on the front. 'Pregnant Sudeten German mother pushed off bicycle by Czech sub-human!'

SOURCE

Description of how Hitler used the newspapers as propaganda before invading Sudeten, Czechoslovakia.

F

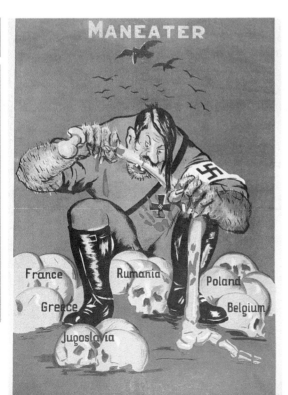

A Russian cartoon from the Second World War.

SOURCE

Goebbels

Joseph Goebbels (1897–1945) became famous as the man who organized German propaganda during the Second World War. He was born in the Rhineland, Germany, and in 1920 became a Doctor of Philosophy at Heidelberg University. In 1922 he joined the Nazi Party and was made Nazi leader of Berlin in 1926. From 1929 he was responsible for organizing Nazi propaganda and in 1930 was elected to the Reichstag. From 1933 to 1945 he held the post of Minister of Enlightenment and Propaganda. This gave him complete control over all forms of communication and expression within Germany. The press was controlled and art, music and literature censored. Goebbels became an expert on the use of radio to convey the Nazi message, and also organized huge rallies, the most spectacular of which were held in Nuremberg.

During the Second World War Goebbels urged the German people to make even greater efforts, but could not prevent Germany's defeat. When he realized that Nazi Germany could not survive he killed his wife and children, before committing suicide in Hitler's bunker.

4.8 Why Did the Allies Win?

In August 1945 the Japanese surrender to the Americans brought the Second World War to an end. Over 37 million people lost their lives in the war, 20 million of them from the USSR. The Allies had won and the Axis powers (Germany, Italy and Japan) had to face the consequences of defeat. Why had that defeat occurred?

It would be easy to decide why the Allies won if we could just say 'the Allied armed forces were better at fighting'. But if that were true, then Germany would not have conquered so much of Europe so easily in 1940. Nor would Japan have taken control of South-East Asia in 1942.

There are of course many reasons why the Allies defeated the Axis powers. Historians often disagree over which were the most important. This unit looks at some of those reasons.

B. Catchpole, 'A Map History of the Modern World', 1982.

From a speech by Winston Churchill in 1940.

A US playing card showing Hitler humiliated by the Soviet giant.

The Hammer and Sickle (the emblem of the USSR) destroys Nazi forces. A British cartoon from January 1943.

E

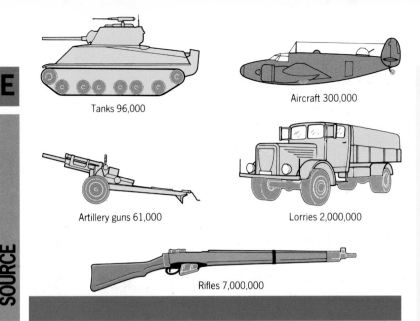

Tanks 96,000

Aircraft 300,000

Artillery guns 61,000

Lorries 2,000,000

Rifles 7,000,000

What America produced for the war 1940–45.

F

In 1941 President Roosevelt organized a scheme called 'lend-lease', by which Britain could borrow or hire military equipment. Many Americans objected to lend-lease, but Roosevelt said that it was just like lending your garden hose to a neighbour whose house was on fire.

A description of the lend-lease system. The USA provided more than $48 billion worth of goods to Britain and the USSR between 1941 and 1945. From C. Culpin, 'Making History', 1984.

G

Yet neither the US fleet, nor US morale was destroyed by the Japanese attack on Pearl Harbor. The USA now declared war on Japan and on Japan's allies, Germany and Italy. Churchill later wrote in his memoirs, 'So we have won after all'.

N. Kelly, 'The Second World War', 1989.

H

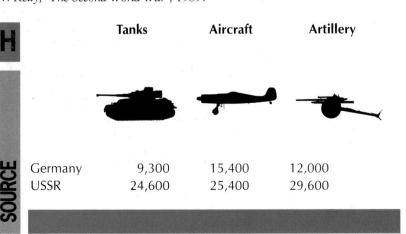

	Tanks	Aircraft	Artillery
Germany	9,300	15,400	12,000
USSR	24,600	25,400	29,600

Production of war goods in 1942.

de Gaulle

Charles de Gaulle (1890–1970) became famous during the Second World War as the leader of the 'Free French' movement. He joined the army at the age of 19 and fought with distinction in the First World War, being wounded at the Battle of Verdun in 1916.

After the First World War he taught at the French Staff College and devoted much of his time to devising military tactics to make maximum use of the new weapons: the tank and air-craft. During the Second World War he was in charge of the armoured division and managed to escape to Britain after the fall of France in 1940. He rallied French morale by leading the 'Free French' and when France was liberated after D-day he led French troops back into Paris.

He became President of France in 1944, but resigned because he felt he had too little power. In 1958 France was faced with a rebellion in its colony, Algeria. De Gaulle was recalled to the Presidency with more extensive powers. During that time he helped France prosper as part of the new 'Common Market' (now the EC). He resigned in 1969.

Franklin Delano Roosevelt

Born: 30 January 1882, Hyde Park, New York, USA
Father: Wealthy landowner
Educated: Groton private school and Harvard University
Married: Anna Eleanor Roosevelt (distant relative) 1905

Career Details:

1907	Began work as lawyer
1910	Elected as Democrat to New York state senate
1912	Appointed assistant secretary of navy
1920	Defeated as candidate for US vice-presidency
1928	Elected Governor of New York
1932	Elected President of the USA
1936	Re-elected President
1940	Re-elected President
1944	Re-elected President

Health Problems: 1921 crippled by poliomyelitis. After three years treatment and exercise regained partial use of legs.

Death: 12 April 1945 as a result of stroke.

Contribution to War Effort:

June 1940	Began providing military supplies to Britain
March 1941	Approved Lend-Lease Act
December 1941	Brought the USA into war

Attended series of conferences with Stalin and Churchill to discuss strategy for winning war 1942
Gave consent to Manhattan Project to develop an atomic bomb

Adolf Hitler

Born: 20 April 1889, Branau am Inn, Austria
Father: Alois Hitler, civil servant
Educated: Local school. (Left at sixteen without qualifications.) Unsuccessful application to attend Vienna Academy of Fine Arts
Married: Eva Braun 29 April 1945

Career Details:

1905–7	Lived at home with mother
1907–13	Lived in poverty in Vienna. Painted postcards and advertising posters
1913	Moved to Munich, Germany
1914	Joined German army. Rose to rank of Corporal. In hospital when war ended
1919	Joined German Worker's Party (later called National Socialist or 'Nazi Party')
1921	Became leader of Nazi Party
1924	Imprisoned following unsuccessful attempt to take over government of Munich
1933	Became Chancellor of Germany

Death: Committed suicide 30 April 1945

Contribution to War Effort:

Rebuilt Germany's armed forces
Brought economic prosperity to Germany in the 1930s
Introduced policy to recover lands lost in Versailles Treaty
Signed agreements with Italy, the USSR and Japan
Responsible for German military strategy in war

Charles Cundall 1945

Joseph Stalin

Born: Tiflis, Georgia, USSR, 21 December 1879
(Real name Joseph Vissarionovich Djugashvili)
Father: Bootmaker
Educated: Local school and priests' training college
(expelled 1899 for being involved in
revolutionary activities)
Married: Ekaterina Svanidze, 1904 (died 1909)
Nadezhda Alliluyeva, 1918 (committed suicide
1932)

Career Details:

1902	Arrested for revolutionary activity and sent into exile in Siberia – escaped
1905–8	Organized bank raids to raise money for revolutionary Bolshevik (later Communist) Party
1917	Became editor of Bolshevik newspaper, *Pravda*
1922	Became Secretary of the Communist Party
1924	Following death of Communist leader, Lenin, Stalin gradually came to control all of the USSR
1941	Became Premier of the USSR

Death: 6 March 1953

Contribution to War Effort:
Began the process of modernizing the USSR to make it more able to defend itself in war
1939 Signed Nazi–Soviet Pact with Germany to buy time to improve Soviet armed forces
1939 Acquired eastern Poland
Took control of military operations against Germany after invasion in 1941
Decision to stay in Moscow when threatened by the Germans increased Soviet people's morale
Took part in wartime conferences with Roosevelt and Churchill to discuss the Allies' tactics

Winston Churchill

Born: Blenheim Palace, Oxford, England
30 November 1874
Father: Lord Randolph Churchill, rich English
landowner
Educated: Harrow School and Sandhurst Military
Academy
Married: Clementine Hozier, 1908

Career Details:
Joined army and took part in Battle of Omdurman 1898
Worked as journalist during Boer War

1900	Became Conservative MP
1904	Joined Liberal Party
1910	Became Home Secretary
1911	Became First Lord of the Admiralty (resigned 1915)
1917	Became Minister for Munitions
1922	Lost seat as MP
1924	Elected as Conservative MP
1924–29	Became Chancellor of the Exchequer
1939	Became First Lord of the Admiralty
1940	Became Prime Minister

Death: 24 January 1965

Contribution to War Effort:
During the 1930s was a bitter critic of Hitler and the policy of appeasement
Put pressure on Chamberlain's government to rearm
Formed War Cabinet to supervise the British war effort
Acted as own Minister of Defence during the war
Kept British morale high during 'darkest hour' of 1940–41 by a series of brilliant patriotic speeches
Took part in wartime conferences with Roosevelt and Stalin to discuss Allies' tactics.

Truman

Harry S. Truman (1884–1972) was the USA's 33rd President. He is particularly famous for authorizing the dropping of the atomic bombs on Hiroshima and Nagasaki in 1945. He first entered politics in the 1920s and in 1935 was elected Senator for the State of Missouri. When Roosevelt won the 1944 Presidential election, Truman was his Vice President.

Truman took office when Roosevelt died in 1945. Shortly after becoming President, he decided that atomic bombs should be dropped on Japan to avoid the cost in US lives of an invasion. After the war he became convinced that there was a Communist threat to world peace and set out the 'Truman Doctrine' against Communism. In 1948 Truman was re-elected in a surprise victory over Thomas Dewey. During his second term he took the USA into the Korean War to try to stop the spread of Communist influence. In 1951 he sacked General MacArthur over a disagreement on how to fight the war. In 1952 he refused to stand again for office.

5.1 A Divided Europe

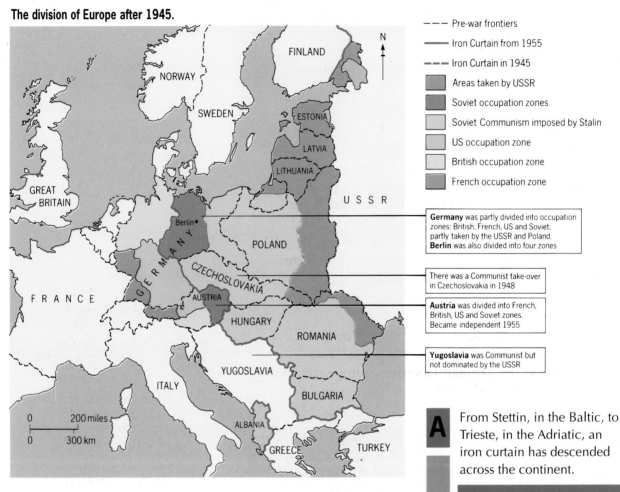

Map legend:
- – – – Pre-war frontiers
- ——— Iron Curtain from 1955
- – – – Iron Curtain in 1945
- Areas taken by USSR
- Soviet occupation zones
- Soviet Communism imposed by Stalin
- US occupation zone
- British occupation zone
- French occupation zone

Germany was partly divided into occupation zones: British, French, US and Soviet; partly taken by the USSR and Poland. **Berlin** was also divided into four zones

There was a Communist take-over in Czechoslovakia in 1948

Austria was divided into French, British, US and Soviet zones. Became independent 1955

Yugoslavia was Communist but not dominated by the USSR

On 7 May 1945 the last German armies surrendered to the Allies. Hitler and Mussolini were both dead. On 17 July the victorious Allies met at **Potsdam** near Berlin. Here they agreed their arrangements for the running of Europe after the war. Earlier in 1945 they had met at **Yalta** in the Crimea and had made a number of important decisions. Germany would be split into four parts, or **zones**, with each zone controlled by one of the allies: Britain, the USA, France and USSR. **Berlin** would also be split into four zones, even though it lay deep in the Soviet zone of Germany. This was because it was the capital.

At Potsdam the Allies agreed that Poland would lose some of its eastern lands to the USSR and make up for this by being given part of Germany. A **United Nations Organization** would be set up to replace the League of Nations. There would be **free elections** in the countries liberated from the Nazis.

A From Stettin, in the Baltic, to Trieste, in the Adriatic, an iron curtain has descended across the continent.

Winston Churchill in a speech at Fulton, USA, in 1946.

B By 1948 all the countries which the USSR controlled had one party governments controlled by the Communists. The Red Army helped Communists take control of the police, the radio and the newspapers. They interfered with elections if they were going against them.

SOURCE

J. Scott, 'The World Since 1914', 1989.

Even before the Potsdam Conference, Stalin had arrested non-Communist politicians in **Poland**. He was determined to control the countries that he had captured from the Germans. Germans were forced out of Poland, Czechoslovakia and Hungary. They were forced to move to Germany. Thousands died on the way. In Germany the Allies, especially the USSR, seized factory machines to help pay for the war.

Now that Germany had been defeated it became clear just how little the Allies had in common. The western democracies thought that the Soviets intended to impose Communism on as many countries as they could, to become more powerful. In 1945 the USSR made sure Communists won the Bulgarian elections. In 1947 Communist governments took power in Hungary and Romania and crushed opposition in Poland. In 1948 they seized power in Czechoslovakia. Other Communists were in control of Yugoslavia and Albania. This frightened the western leaders.

In 1947 the President of the USA, **Truman**, made it clear that he would oppose any further spread of Communism. This became known as the **Truman Doctrine**. Europe was divided by politics and distrust. A **'Cold War'** was beginning.

C

SOURCE

As early as 1941 Stalin had made it clear that the USSR would only permit friendly countries on its borders. He remarked that twice in 30 years the USSR had been invaded through an unfriendly Poland.

L. Snellgrove, 'The Modern World Since 1870', 1981.

Tito

Josip Broz (1892–1980), known as Tito, became famous as leader of the Yugoslavian partisans during the Second World War. In the First World War he fought in the Austrian army and became a prisoner of war in Russia. He stayed to fight for the Bolsheviks (Communists) in the civil war. Tito returned to Yugoslavia in 1920, but was imprisoned for six years as a Communist agitator. In 1941 the Germans occupied Yugoslavia and Tito organized the resistance movement against them. At the end of the war he became Prime Minister of Yugoslavia. In 1953 he was made President and held that office until his death in 1980.

D

SOURCE

Leading Nazis were put on trial for their 'war crimes'. The most famous trials were held in Nuremburg. Many of those responsible, though, were never brought to justice.

5.2 The United Nations Organization

In 1941 Churchill and Roosevelt made an agreement called the **Atlantic Charter**. In it they set out their aims: the British Empire should not gain any more colonies; countries liberated during the war should be free to run themselves; world living conditions should be improved; people should be free to travel; weapons of war should be reduced.

In January 1942, 26 nations signed the **Declaration of the United Nations**, which meant they agreed with the ideas of the Atlantic Charter. In 1944 Britain, China, the USA and the USSR began planning a new organization to encourage peaceful cooperation between countries. This would replace the failed League of Nations.

The idea was discussed again at the Allied meeting at Yalta in January 1945. In April, representatives of 50 nations met in San Francisco. After discussions they signed the **United Nations Charter** which set out the ideas of the new organization.

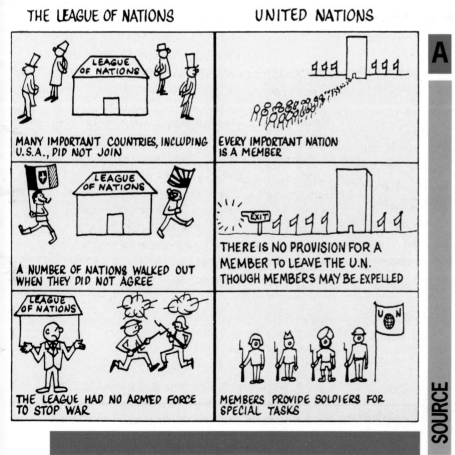

THE LEAGUE OF NATIONS   UNITED NATIONS

MANY IMPORTANT COUNTRIES, INCLUDING U.S.A., DID NOT JOIN

EVERY IMPORTANT NATION IS A MEMBER

A NUMBER OF NATIONS WALKED OUT WHEN THEY DID NOT AGREE

THERE IS NO PROVISION FOR A MEMBER TO LEAVE THE U.N. THOUGH MEMBERS MAY BE EXPELLED

THE LEAGUE HAD NO ARMED FORCE TO STOP WAR

MEMBERS PROVIDE SOLDIERS FOR SPECIAL TASKS

A

SOURCE

Comparing the UN and the League, from P. Moss, 'History Alive', 1977.

The UN is organized differently from the League of Nations. The representatives of member countries meet in the **General Assembly**. A two-thirds majority is needed to agree a decision. Most decisions are in the hands of a **Security Council**. In 1945 this had five permanent members (Britain, China, France, USA, USSR) and six temporary members. The number of temporary members was increased to ten after 1965. Each temporary member is only on the Council for two years.

The Security Council meets throughout the year and its decisions apply to all members of the UN. The permanent members have the **right of veto**. This means that if one of them votes against an idea, that idea cannot be passed. The aim of this was to make sure that any decision had the support of all the major countries of the world.

The Security Council has a large group of people to carry out its decisions. Their work is overseen by the **Secretary General**. The first was a Norwegian, **Trygve Lie**.

The United Nations Organization has set up a huge number of different committees and agencies to carry out its work. These include the **Court of International Justice**, which was taken over from the League of Nations; the **Food and Agriculture Organization (FAO)** which helps improve farming and protect natural resources; the **UN Education, Scientific and Cultural Organization (UNESCO)** which encourages education and understanding between nations; the **World Health Organization (WHO)** helping to improve world health; the **UN Relief and Rehabilitation Administration (UNRRA)** and the **International Refugee Organization (IRO)** which helps refugees.

At the end of the war the UN also played a part in helping to organize loans to countries to help them rebuild their economies again.

D

SOURCE

The League failed for two reasons. First, powerful countries like the USA and Germany after 1933 were not members. Second, it could only ask members to take action to keep peace.

The UN avoided the first of these weaknesses. All the Allies agreed to join and later on so did the defeated countries. But the second weakness was harder to avoid. Governments were not likely to give up national power by letting the new world organization have much power of its own.

J. Scott, 'The World Since 1914', 1989.

Hammarskjöld

Dag Hammarskjöld (1905–61) was a Professor of Economics at Stockholm University in Sweden and a member of the Swedish government, before becoming a delegate to the United Nations (UN). When the first UN Secretary-General, Trygve Lie, retired in 1953 Hammarskjöld took his place. He was re-elected to the post in 1957. Hammarskjöld had many problems to deal with during his time as Secretary-General, and won great support for his determination to show that the UN could play a significant role in helping to maintain world peace. In 1956 there was a serious crisis in the Middle East when the British invaded Egypt and took over the Suez Canal. Hammarskjöld played a major part in persuading the British to withdraw. After this he made many attempts to find a peaceful solution to the problems in the Middle East. In 1960–61 serious fighting broke out in the Belgium Congo. Hammarskjöld flew to Africa to try to resolve the dispute. He was killed when his plane crashed over Zambia.

5.3 Refugees

Refugees are people who have been forced to leave their homes. This can be because of war, or some kind of natural disaster. During the twentieth century many thousands of people have become refugees as a result of warfare. At the end of the Second World War hundreds of thousands of people found themselves without a home.

Many people had their homes destroyed by fighting and were forced to escape with the few belongings that they could carry. Others were forced to leave their homes because they were hated because of their nationality. Jews who survived the Nazi extermination camps often ended up thousands of miles from their original homes. Between 1945 and 1947 the liberated countries of eastern Europe expelled over 16 million Germans who lived in their countries. One in eight died as they were forced to flee westward. During the war the Germans and Japanese had made thousands of people work as **forced labour**. When the war ended these people were left far from home. In Japan, US bombing had destroyed thousands of homes. In China the war had disrupted civilian life for eight years. All these refugees were in danger from hunger, cold, disease and the cruelty of other people.

As early as 1943 the western Allies set up plans for helping refugees. They set up the **International Refugee Organization** and later the **United Nations Relief and Rehabilitation Administration (UNRRA)**. They worked behind the front lines and continued their work when the war ended. They provided temporary homes in Refugee Camps and food and clothing. They helped people get back to where their homes had been, or set up a new life elsewhere. Much of the money to do this work was provided by the USA. After the war, in 1947, the Americans provided even more money to help rebuild the economies of countries wrecked by the war. This was called **Marshall Aid**. As well as providing help, the USA aimed to stop the spread of Communism into these countries.

The evidence in this unit explains why so many people were made refugees as a result of the Second World War and what life was like for some of these men, women and children.

A SOURCE

Berlin is a city of desolation and shattered dreams, inhabited by a half mad, half starving population, clawing its way into battered food shops, slinking for shelter into cellars and begging favours from the victors.

Soviet officer, 1945.

B SOURCE

Sowing of crops in many battle stricken areas is impossible this year. The food production will, for some time, be below the pre-war level.

Statement by representatives of Britain, USA and Canada following the Washington Conference on Problems of World Supplies and Distribution, 30 April 1945.

C SOURCE

Millions of Germans, Danzigers and Sudetenlanders are now on the move. Groups will take to the road, trek hundreds of miles and lose half their numbers through disease or exhaustion.

'Manchester Guardian', November 1945.

Chinese refugees in 1946.

SOURCE

Marshall

George Marshall (1880–1959) was a US army officer and statesman. He was Army Chief of Staff in the Second World War and Secretary of State in Truman's government after the war. He strongly supported Truman's anti-Communist policy and thought that Communism flourished best where there was poverty and suffering. Because much of Europe was suffering the economic effects of world war, he thought there was a danger that Communism could take root. It was, therefore, the duty of the USA to provide economic aid. As Marshall himself said in 1947, 'The truth of the matter is that Europe's requirements for the next three or four years are so much greater than her present ability to pay that she must have substantial help.'

Marshall therefore devised the Marshall Plan which made available $15,000 million in aid for post-war reconstruction. Sixteen nations took advantage of the aid that the USA was offering. As a result of this plan Marshall was awarded the Nobel Peace Prize in 1953.

E

SOURCE

Throughout history, warfare has led to the mistreatment of those civilians unfortunate enough to live within the areas of fighting. Often villages were destroyed and civilians slaughtered; sometimes the fighting disrupted food production and the civilians starved to death. The Second World War, however, brought changes in the way that warfare was conducted. From now on civilians would increasingly become targets for attack. The Blitz, the Allied bombing of Germany and the US air raids on Japan, took a terrible toll in human lives.

In addition came the losses through disease, starvation and homelessness.

N. Kelly, 'The Second World War', 1989.

F

SOURCE

The Japanese occupied vast areas of the Far East and their treatment of native populations was relatively humane. But Hitler's Third Reich based its economy on the employment of slave labour in the factories, mines and on the land. Thus in the Second World War the Germans were responsible for shifting many nationalities all over Europe. There was little happiness for 'refugees' and 'displaced persons'. Some fled westwards to escape the advancing Red Army; others, liberated by British and US troops, tried to find their way home.

B. Catchpole, 'A Map History of the Modern World', 1982.